Principles for Living in Line with God's Word

Shelley Helton

All emphasis within Scripture is the author's own.

Paperback ISBN: 978-1-66781-230-4
eBook ISBN: 978-1-66781-231-1

CONTENTS

PREFACE

THIS BOOK IS DEDICATED TO THOSE WHO LOVE GOD WITH all their hearts but feel that something is missing. They struggle with conflict, loss, anxiety, and fear, while others experience breakthroughs, provision, and wholeness. How is it possible that God's people could have such radically different outcomes? It boils down to how we understand God's Word.

The sad fact is that many churches aren't teaching the full counsel of God. There are prosperity preachers who seem to focus only on money. The bulk of their message implies that if you give enough, it will solve all your problems. Yet, if that's the case, why are some people struggling financially while the preacher lives in splendor? You give and give, but nothing good ever happens to you. You remain stuck in the same sad cycle of poverty year after year.

Some preachers teach that women must never wear pants, men must grow their beards to a certain length, and children are never to watch television. People are to be suffering servants, and anything less means a one-way trip to Hell.

How is a Christian to make sense of all this? The solution requires a return to the Word of God. True happiness lies in the full counsel of God, yet many churches aren't teaching their people how to live the life God intended. What's missing is practical instruction on how to do what Jesus said to do. This book provides straightforward guidance on topics that are missing from the messages being preached in today's pulpits. It's time to get back to basics. The Bible stands on its own as the source of truth for everything, so you should consult it first for every issue you face. You don't need to spend thousands of dollars on counseling when your Bible is within arm's reach. You can find the answer to every question within its pages, so stop looking elsewhere for answers.

The latest guru can't help you. Most of them teach from a secular perspective, or there are elements of secular teaching mixed in with their Biblical teaching. Others focus on New Age concepts. Instead, everything must come from a Biblical foundation.

Sports figures, celebrities, and pop stars make a lot of money to entertain people, but they aren't heroes. Far from it. They didn't suffer and die for you the way Jesus did. He's the one who deserves your adoration and praise. He's the one you should seek to emulate.

Living a life that pleases God isn't easy. You'll be surprised at what the Bible reveals about God's formula for a successful life. It will require sacrifice, but it's the least you can do to serve Him. You won't always get your way. He may ask you to give up some things to serve Him the way He wants. What will probably stand out most is the price you'll pay if you want to go the distance with Him, because it <u>will</u> cost you. But is the price worth it? Yes! Read this book with eternity in mind, because God's heart is always on people. He wants great things for you, but He wants you to do it His way. In John 14:15, Jesus said that if you love Him, you'll keep His commandments. Most people think that God's commands are limited to the Ten Commandments, but that's not true.

You'll find examples throughout this book of God's commands and practical tips for how you can apply the principles to your own life. You'll read about Abraham, the three Hebrew boys, Joseph, Daniel, David, the

Apostle Paul, and last but not least, Jesus. He sets the ultimate example of how to live life abundantly with integrity and passion. He ran His race to the fullest and pleased His Father. He modeled the perfect life and set the perfect example.

We'll look at numerous verses of Scripture throughout this study, but one stands out as the foundational Scripture - Matthew 6:33.

"But seek ye first the kingdom of God, and his righteousness; and all these things shall be added unto you."
(Matthew 6:33, KJV 1900)

Seeking God's kingdom first means that He takes first place in every area of your life. You can't cut corners and expect to get away with it. Putting Him first changes everything. It leads to a relationship with Him that alters every aspect of your life for the better. It's how you can live life the way He intended.

Put what you've learned into practice when you reach the end of this study. Please don't let it gather dust on the bookshelf: Let it serve as a spiritual boot camp. You can be more and do more than you ever thought possible, but you have to do it with Jesus as your central focus, because all things are possible with Him.

Chapter One:
Seek First The Kingdom

SUCCESS FROM GOD'S PERSPECTIVE HAPPENS ONLY BY SEEK-ing first His kingdom, but many people don't know what that really means. Many people think that as long as they go to church and live right most of the time, then that means they are seeking first His Kingdom. However, that would be a superficial understanding. Matthew 6:33 gives us the clue to success.

"But seek first the Kingdom of God and His righteousness,
and all these things shall be added to you."
(Matthew 6:33, NKJV)

One of the first things to note is the word 'kingdom,' which refers to a domain, a place, or a piece of geography ruled by a monarch. Therefore, referring to the Kingdom of God speaks of a territory where God rules and reigns. That territory, for believers, is our hearts and minds. We know that because Jesus said in Luke 17:20-21 that the Kingdom of God is in us.

Thus, when we talk about the Kingdom of God, we're talking about God reigning over us. This means that, just like the ruler of any kingdom, past or present, there are things the ruler approves of and things he doesn't. This is also the case with God. Many people in today's culture have changed the Word of God to fit the lifestyle they've chosen for themselves, but the Bible has clear standards that are not changeable with the times. If He calls it sin, so must we. We must model our lives after His Word, not try to change it to fit our lifestyles. A lot of compromise occurs in the world today, but it's not excused by God. If the Bible says it's a sin, it's a sin. Simple as that.

People have argued with me about that. They'll say that I'm intolerant if I hold to a Biblical view. They'll say they disagree with my beliefs. But let's be clear: It's not really me they have an issue with. What they're really saying is that they have an issue with God's Word. They want me to support their viewpoint, as if that would somehow make it okay, but I can't do that. If I do, I've compromised, and if I compromise, then I can no longer say that God is ruling and reigning in my life.

Jesus said something in James 4:4 that speaks to compromise.

> "*You adulterous people! Do you not know that friendship with the world is enmity with God? Therefore whoever wishes to be a friend of the world makes himself an enemy of God.*"
> (James 4:4, ESV)

If you compromise your beliefs to keep your friends or to be popular, or for any other reason, then you have chosen friendship with the world, which opposes the purposes of God. Friends, it doesn't get much clearer than that.

Let's look at another Scripture if this one doesn't convince you.

> "*Love not the world, neither the things that are in the world. If any man love the world, the love of the Father is*

not in him."
(1 John 2:15, KJV 1900)

If God is ruling in your life, it means not only that you're doing things His way but also that you're doing things His way all the time. Here are some questions we need to answer to know for sure whether or not He's ruling and reigning.

Does He have access to all aspects of your life?

Does He have a say in what you do, where you live, where you work, who you marry, and how you spend your time? If He doesn't, then He's not ruling and reigning in your life.

If we look closely at our lives, can we say we're really seeking first His kingdom? If God doesn't have the final say in every aspect of our lives, then we can't say that we're seeking first His kingdom. God must have total control over every aspect of our lives if He is to rule and reign there. Here are some ways to know when you're not seeking first His kingdom:

- If you take a higher paying job for the money when you know God wants you to stay where you are, then you're not seeking first His kingdom.

- If you know God has spoken to you about the mate He's chosen for you, yet you date others because you don't want to wait, that's not seeking first the Kingdom of God.

- If you focus on your child's sports activities instead of making sure they go to church, then you're not seeking first the kingdom.

- If you refuse to apologize to your spouse when the Lord has directed you to do so because you feel you weren't in the wrong, then you're not seeking first the kingdom.

- If you remain living where you are even though you know the Lord has directed you to move somewhere else, then you're not seeking first His kingdom.

- If you've not given money to a ministry because you want to use it for something else, even though you know God laid it on your heart to give, then you're not seeking first the Kingdom of God.

- If you compromise your beliefs because you don't want to stand up and defend what the Word of God says about a matter, then you're not seeking first His kingdom.

- If you refuse to obey the principles found in the Word of God, then you're not seeking first His kingdom.

- If you continue to use debt, though God has laid it on your heart to pay off your bills so you can live debt free, then you're not seeking first the kingdom.

- If you maintain ungodly friendships because you want to be popular at school or at work, then you cannot say that you're seeking first the kingdom.

The list of 'ifs' could go on and on, but I'm sure you get the point. Each of us must determine for ourselves whether we're truly seeking first the kingdom. It's an important question for us to answer, because there are many people who will discover that they aren't allowing God to rule and reign, which means that they don't qualify for the second half of the verse that says, "and all these things shall be added."

What does it mean when it says, "and all these things shall be added"? It's the benefit that comes from putting the Kingdom first. All these things that people sweat and labor to acquire are things that God will add to us.

We don't add it to ourselves: He does it. That's His part of the agreement, and it was His idea, not ours. He'll give us everything we need for our lives if we focus on His kingdom. He'll focus on our business if we focus on His. He'll add all of those things we need without us having to worry about it. Remember that this Scripture states it shall be added to us. It is not us adding it to ourselves.

But many people find their lives don't match up to what this verse promises. Stuff isn't being added to them like they thought. They eke out a living, but that's about it. It's a daily struggle to pay bills, and they worry about what would happen if a financial emergency hit. They never get ahead, or if they are getting ahead, they're having to do things they know are contrary to God's Word.

There might be some people who still don't believe they need to put God first, to seek His kingdom first. Their lives are moving along just fine, and they don't feel the need to change. If that describes you, keep in mind that if God isn't reigning in your life, someone else is, and he's not the one you want governing your life. I'll say it again: You're either being ruled by God or you're being ruled by the enemy. You get to choose, so choose wisely.

> *"I call heaven and earth as witnesses today against you, that I have set before you life and death, blessing and cursing; therefore choose life, that both you and your descendants may live;"*
> (Deuteronomy 30:19, NKJV)

While you get to choose between life and death, God is giving you the answer right here in this verse, so make the right decision. Yes, seeking first the Kingdom of God will cost you, but it's worth the effort. I'll say more about this in a later chapter.

Many God-fearing, churchgoing people unwittingly violate the requirement to put God first, then they wonder why things aren't working out. Remember that the Word also says that God's people are destroyed because of a lack of knowledge (Hosea 4:6). The knowledge is available by reading God's Word, but many people don't take the time to read it and understand the requirements. I know people who carry Bibles to church but never bother to open them; they're there for show. This doesn't help you. The Bible can change your life, but it won't do you any good unless you open it, read it, and apply the principles.

Evaluate your life to determine who's reigning there. It's easy enough to make the needed adjustments to ensure that God is in control if you find you're being ruled by the enemy, but <u>you</u> must make the adjustments. God won't force you: He gave every man and woman the gift of free will, so it's up to us to decide. You must pray for forgiveness and get back on track. Once you can honestly say that you're seeking first the kingdom, then the rest of the verse applies to you. Understand that things won't change overnight. You didn't get into a mess overnight, so the fix won't happen overnight, either. God is faithful: If you take the steps to align your life with His Word and give Him complete control, then He is faithful to provide what you need.

Chapter Two: God Is My Source

THIS CHAPTER EXAMINES WHAT IT MEANS FOR GOD TO BE our provider. Too many people rely on their jobs, their parents, the government, or some other source to provide what they need to live, but that is a grave mistake. God wants to be our everything. He wants to be the One we look to as our source of supply.

Placing their trust in God to supply all their needs is one of the hardest things to learn for many Christians. That was the case for me, but once I took the leap of faith and experienced the results, I've never gone back. I can honestly say that God has never let me down.

Throughout this chapter, I'll explain how it worked for me so you can achieve similar results.

Before we begin, I'd like us to look at a key verse of Scripture found in Proverbs 3:5,6.

> *"Trust in the Lord with all your heart, and do not lean on your own understanding. In all your ways acknowledge*

him, and he will make straight your paths."
(Proverbs 3:5–6, ESV)

Trusting the Lord with every fiber of your being is not for the faint of heart, because it will challenge everything you've ever known. Many of us have been taught to depend on ourselves because we could trust nobody else. But God is not like any human: He is always worthy of our trust, and He cannot lie under any set of circumstances.

"*God is not a man, that he should lie; Neither the son of man, that he should repent: Hath he said, and shall he not do it? Or hath he spoken, and shall he not make it good?*"
(Numbers 23:19, KJV 1900)

However, the question remains: How do I learn to trust God as my source for everything, especially when I cannot see Him? The first thing I did was to read Scriptures on the subject. There are so many that it would occupy a lot of space to include them all here, so I've listed the main ones I use.

Read these several times a day. Read them aloud whenever you can because faith comes by hearing (Romans 10:17).

"*Thus saith the Lord; Cursed be the man that trusteth in man, and maketh flesh his arm, and whose heart departeth from the Lord.*"
(Jeremiah 17:5, KJV 1900)

"*But thou shalt remember the Lord thy God: for it is he that giveth thee power to get wealth, that he may establish his covenant which he sware unto thy fathers, as it is this day.*"
(Deuteronomy 8:18, KJV 1900)

"And my God shall supply all your need according to His riches in glory by Christ Jesus."
(Philippians 4:19, NKJV)

"Yahweh is my shepherd; I will not lack for anything."
(Psalm 23:1, LEB)

"Command those who are rich in this present age not to be proud and not to put their hope in the uncertainty of riches, but in God, who provides us all things richly for enjoyment,"
(1 Timothy 6:17, LEB)

"The young lions lack and suffer hunger; But those who seek the LORD shall not lack any good thing."
(Psalm 34:10, NKJV)

"He hath given meat unto them that fear him: He will ever be mindful of his covenant."
(Psalm 111:5, KJV 1900)

I absorbed these verses into my heart. What do I mean by this? I mean I could eventually quote them from memory. I meditated on them continually.

I went to the Lord for my answer from that point forward whenever a need arose. I prayed about the situation and let the Holy Spirit guide me, according to Proverbs 3:5,6. People often ask how to tell if you're being led by the Holy Spirit. It's not as difficult as it sounds.

After I've prayed, I wait on the Lord. Waiting on the Lord means I sit before Him to hear what He has to say about the situation. This isn't necessarily a five-minute proposition. Sometimes, I'll sit quietly for ten or twenty minutes before I hear something. As I wait, I might get an impression that I need to do something, or He might give me a verse of Scripture to follow. From that point, I take action on what I heard. Remember: faith without works is dead (James 2:17).

The following story is a real-life example of how it worked for me.

Many years ago, my husband and I wanted to build a house. Deep down, I wanted to avoid the hassle of building the house, but I thought it was the only way to ensure we got what we wanted. We also thought we had identified a perfect piece of property that a relative owned. The lot was across the street from that relative, and my husband and I thought that was a good thing.

I prayed and asked God for that property, according to Mark 11:24,25, and I believed I had received. I asked Him for the specific house I wanted, which was a certain amount of square footage, on a large lot, with granite countertops and an open floor plan. I wanted the house to be in a suitable area, with high property values and low crime. The lot across from my relative seemed to fit the bill.

From the moment I prayed that prayer, I felt uneasy but couldn't tie it to anything in particular. I just knew that something didn't feel right, but I made an offer for the property to put my faith into action. My relative agreed to sell it, but I couldn't get rid of the uneasiness I felt. The feeling wouldn't go away, so we retracted the offer.

Right after that happened, my husband decided we should go house hunting just to see what was on the market. We got in our truck and drove around. There was one area my husband wanted to check out, but I said that I didn't want to bother. He said that he saw some balloons on a sign showing an open house and we should go look.

We drove down the street to see the house, and it was gorgeous. It was everything we wanted. When we stepped inside the house, my husband got excited because it even had the granite countertops and the open floor plan we desired. He wanted to make an offer right away, but I wanted to ensure I had the Lord's blessing on it before we moved forward with an offer.

I stepped outside to pray, but the moment I did, I could hear the Lord say, deep down in my spirit, "This is the house." We made the offer, but I dropped the offer price because I didn't want to pay what the owner was asking. I didn't even consult my husband before doing this, though I thought I was doing the right thing. Our offer was rejected, and my husband was heartbroken.

I had that uneasy feeling again after we went home. I prayed about it, and the Lord's reply was a stunning rebuke. He said, "I never told you to drop the price." I asked Him to help me correct the situation, and here's what He did.

The next day was a workday, so I didn't have any plans to contact the real estate agent until my lunch break. But before I could do that, I received a call from a friend who said that he found a house he thought we'd like. I asked him where it was. It was the same house. I explained to him what I'd done. He laughed and said he could take care of it with a phone call because he knew the owners. He asked what we intended to offer, and I replied we would offer the full price. We received a call back within a few hours that they accepted our offer. Our real estate agent replied that we almost lost the house. Two other couples had made offers, and the owner was getting ready to accept one of them.

The end of the story is that we bought the house we wanted, and it was perfect for us in every way. It is a sanctuary for us and we have the best neighbors anyone could want, so we got the best end of the deal. I've never regretted that God gave me that uneasy feeling about my relative's property because I know it would have been a mistake. I'm so grateful that He took me on a detour to the place that I really wanted.

If you encounter situations when your prayers aren't being answered exactly as you think they should, take the situation before the Lord. If He tells you to trust Him, that's exactly what you should do. Give Him credit for knowing what the right answer should be. If you'll stand in faith, God will give you better than what you asked for, but that's only if you'll let Him lead you. Take Proverbs 3:5,6 to heart and let Him lead you in the way you should go. We don't know the future, but we know the God who does. Trust Him to give you His best.

I also recommend that you trust God to answer your prayers at the time that's best for you. There will be times when it seems the answer isn't coming, but God is never late. He supplies the answer when it is needed.

Never tell God how you want your prayer answered. Yes, we are to ask God specifically for what we want, but we don't have the option of determining how He answers. That's within His jurisdiction, not ours. Don't limit Him to your plans and purposes, because that never works. He is in charge, and we should trust His methods. We see examples of weird methods throughout the entire Bible. God loves to surprise people.

In John 9, we read the miracle of Jesus healing a blind man.

"And as he went away, he saw a man blind from birth. And his disciples asked him, saying, "Rabbi, who sinned, this man or his parents, that he should be born blind?" Jesus replied, "Neither this man sinned nor his parents, but it happened so that the works of God could be revealed in him. It is necessary for us to do the deeds of the one who sent me while it is day; night is coming, when no one can work! While I am in the world, I am the light of the world." When he had said these things, he spat on the ground and made clay with the saliva, and smeared the clay on his eyes. And he said to him, "Go, wash in the pool of Siloam" (which is translated "sent"). So he went and washed and came back seeing."

(John 9:1–7, LEB)

Imagine what would have happened if the man had said, "Lord, that's gross; heal me some other way." We probably wouldn't be reading about him today.

Jesus tells Peter to go fishing in yet another account. The first fish he takes up would have a coin in its mouth. That was to be used to pay the taxes for Peter and Jesus.

> *"And when they were come to Capernaum, they that received tribute money came to Peter, and said, Doth not your master pay tribute? He saith, Yes. And when he was come into the house, Jesus prevented him, saying, What thinkest thou, Simon? of whom do the kings of the earth take custom or tribute? of their own children, or of strangers? Peter saith unto him, Of strangers. Jesus saith unto him, Then are the children free. Notwithstanding, lest we should offend them, go thou to the sea, and cast an hook, and take up the fish that first cometh up; and when thou hast opened his mouth, thou shalt find a piece of money: that take, and give unto them for me and thee."*
> (Matthew 17:24–27, KJV 1900)

If the Lord tells you to do something, just do it. Don't make excuses for why you can't do it. Be obedient and you'll see Him do things in your life that will astound you. However, if you refuse to take the steps that God tells you to take, then you'll live without the provision He wants to give you.

Remember that God only has good intentions toward His children. Many people have fathers who are not good examples of what a father should be. They judge God according to the examples their fathers set, but we should never judge God by how humans act.

"The Lord is good to all: And his tender mercies are over all his works."
(Psalm 145:9, KJV 1900)

"So Jesus said to him, "Why do you call me good? No one is good except God alone."
(Mark 10:18, LEB)

"Taste and see that Yahweh is good; blessed is the man who takes refuge in him."
(Psalm 34:8, LEB)

These are just a few of the verses you can find on the goodness of God. Meditate on His goodness. You can be set free to trust Him with every aspect of your life once you're convinced of that goodness. He is the source of every good thing. Allow Him to be your source and you'll see how good life truly can be.

Chapter Three:
Authority Of The Believer

ONE OF THE LEAST UNDERSTOOD TOPICS IN CHRISTIANITY today is spiritual authority. Most Christians don't even know they have it. They suffer day by day under demonic attack and just sit back and take it, yet they've been dealing with a defeated foe the entire time. I'll say it again: Satan is a defeated foe. Jesus laid waste to his kingdom when He arose from the dead.

Here's the thing about authority. You can have it, but it's exactly the same as not having it if you don't exercise it. Believers must exercise their authority for it to work. Many times, we think other people are our problems, but the Bible tells us something different.

> *"For we wrestle not against flesh and blood, but against principalities, against powers, against the rulers of the darkness of this world, against spiritual wickedness in high places."*
> *(Ephesians 6:12, KJV 1900)*

Your issue is never with other people. Your issue is only ever with the unseen realm affecting the lives of others. Still, Satan is a defeated foe. You're waging war with someone who has already lost the battle. Thus, the question is: How do we enforce the authority Jesus has given us? I'm glad you asked.

Jesus gave us the right to use His Name when He died on the cross and rose from the dead. That's right. We can use His Name. There is nothing more powerful than that Name. There's a verse of Scripture that I'd like you to memorize. Study it until you can remember it by heart, because it's the directive from our Lord and Savior, Jesus Christ, to tread on the enemy. He gave us the power over the enemy. But He requires us to take that authority, that power, and use it.

"Behold, I give unto you power to tread on serpents and scorpions, and over all the power of the enemy: and nothing shall by any means hurt you."
(Luke 10:19, KJV 1900)

There's another Scripture that I want to bring to your attention right now.

"My people are destroyed for lack of knowledge; because you have rejected knowledge, I reject you from acting as a priest for me. And since you have forgotten the law of your God, I will also forget your children."
(Hosea 4:6, LEB)

God's children are constantly being destroyed because of a lack of knowledge. Knowledge is everywhere. Knowledge only increases as time goes by, yet Christians continually suffer the onslaught of the enemy. This is wrong, very wrong. Jesus gave us the authority to trample on the enemy, yet we do nothing more than take it. We don't fight back. We give up and give in. Why? Lack of knowledge.

What is authority? It is delegated power. I'm going to take a quick detour to illustrate the concept of authority. Let's say that you're a police officer and you catch somebody speeding on the freeway. You turn on your flashing lights and give chase. The person pulls the car over not because you had the personal strength to make him or her do so, but because you had the authority that was delegated to you when you became a police officer.

You can't make Satan back off in the spirit realm because of your own personal power. You can make him back off because of the authority of the Name of Jesus and the fact that Jesus delegated it to you when you became a child of God. But again, none of this does you any good unless you recognize that you have the authority and enforce your rights.

The Name of Jesus is above every name. Everything above the earth, on the earth, and under the earth is subject to it.

"Therefore God also has highly exalted Him and given Him the name which is above every name,"
(Philippians 2:9, NKJV)

"Then the seventy returned with joy, saying, "Lord, even the demons are subject to us in Your name.""
(Luke 10:17, NKJV)

That Name is more powerful than you can imagine. Think about it: The demons were subject to the seventy just by the use of the Name. That should tell you it truly is above all names. But here's the point I'm trying to make: You don't have to fear anything if you know who you are and Whose you are. His Name is yours to use in time of need if you've made Jesus your Lord and Savior.

That said, I caution people against using that Name in vain. And, for the record, using His Name in vain isn't just about using it as a cuss word; it's so much more than that. It's treating the Name as though it's worth nothing. People who use the Lord's Name casually, as though it's worthless, are using the Lord's Name in vain.

Let's step back and look at Psalm 91:14 again with this in mind.

""Because he has set his love upon Me,
therefore I will deliver him; I will set him on high,
because he has known My name."
(Psalm 91:14, NKJV)

God will deliver and set on high those who know His Name. But you can't know His Name unless you know His Word. This is one reason there are so many powerless Christians in the world. They figure that as long as they go to church every week, they're covered. But they're not. If you don't open the Word of God and study it, you have no way to appropriate His promises for yourself. You can't appropriate what you don't know you have.

God made His ways and nature available to us to understand, but many people don't take the time to read His Word. They read a few verses every week during church service, but that's it. The rest of the time, the Bible lies on the coffee table gathering dust, and that's a shame.

Recognizing that the Lord's Name has power in it is one way you can honor it. Never use it lightly or as though it has no meaning, because it's a nuclear bomb to the enemy. That Name sets people free from demonic possession and oppression, and it provides protection in time of need. If you take the time to know the Name, then it will ensure you're safe even in the worst of times.

Study the 91st Psalm like your life depends on it, because it could come to that one day. You don't want to be in a dangerous situation with no protection. You never have to fear if you know that Name and the power in it. Philippians 2:9-11 says that Name is higher than everything above, on, or under the earth. Proverbs 18:10 says the Name is a strong tower.

I'll give you a real-life example of the power of the Name of Jesus. Not too long ago, someone came to me in distress because he hadn't been sleeping well. He'd told me he couldn't remember the last time he'd slept well, and it was affecting his health and his marriage. Medical doctors couldn't find anything wrong. He didn't know what to do.

After we talked for a while, I realized he was dealing with a demon. He was being demonized and didn't realize it. Before I go any further, I'd like to mention that people spend a lot of time debating whether someone is oppressed or possessed. Those kinds of debates waste a lot of time in my humble opinion. This man was dealing with a demon and he needed help right away, otherwise his health and marriage would continue to suffer.

I took authority over the demon in the Name of Jesus and commanded it to leave. It departed, and he slept soundly from that point. I taught him how to take that same authority for himself so he doesn't need me to take care of it for him. It's simple to do if you understand the power of the Name. You have the authority.

Unfortunately, churches teach little on the authority the believer has in the Name of Jesus, which is a travesty. So much power is available, but Christians are walking around with no knowledge of it. Believers are being tormented by the enemy and don't even know they have the power to do something about it.

If you're reading this and are not a believer, then don't use the Name, because you have no authority to do so. There is an account in the Bible of the seven sons of Sceva that should make my point clear.

> *"And God wrought special miracles by the hands of Paul: So that from his body were brought unto the sick handkerchiefs or aprons, and the diseases departed from them, and the evil spirits went out of them. Then certain of the vagabond Jews, exorcists, took upon them to call over them which had evil spirits the name of the Lord Jesus,*

saying, We adjure you by Jesus whom Paul preacheth. And there were seven sons of one Sceva, a Jew, and chief of the priests, which did so. And the evil spirit answered and said, Jesus I know, and Paul I know; but who are ye? And the man in whom the evil spirit was leaped on them, and overcame them, and prevailed against them, so that they fled out of that house naked and wounded. And this was known to all the Jews and Greeks also dwelling at Ephesus; and fear fell on them all, and the name of the Lord Jesus was magnified. And many that believed came, and confessed, and shewed their deeds. Many of them also which used curious arts brought their books together, and burned them before all men: and they counted the price of them, and found it fifty thousand pieces of silver. So mightily grew the word of God and prevailed."

(Acts 19:11–20, KJV 1900)

However, if you're a child of God, then the authority granted to Jesus by God Almighty (Matthew 28:18) was delegated to you (Mark 16:17-18).

"And Jesus approached and spoke to them, saying, "All authority in heaven and on earth has been given to me."

(Matthew 28:18, LEB)

"And these signs shall follow them that believe; In my name shall they cast out devils; they shall speak with new tongues; They shall take up serpents; and if they drink any deadly thing, it shall not hurt them; they shall lay hands on the sick, and they shall recover."

(Mark 16:17–18, KJV 1900)

Let's look at the practical application of the authority granted to the believer with this background in mind.

One of the first things I'd like to re-emphasize is that you're either yielding to God or you're yielding to Satan. There's nothing in between. It's your decision and you must make it continually. Let me say it again: It's your decision.

"I call heaven and earth to record this day against you, that I have set before you life and death, blessing and cursing: therefore choose life, that both thou and thy seed may live:"
(Deuteronomy 30:19, KJV 1900)

Making the right decision comes with a price, and the question is whether you're willing to pay it. You must come under the authority of Jesus if you want to walk in the authority of that Name effectively. Many people think they can throw the Name of Jesus around and it'll accomplish everything they want. But such is not the case. You won't be able to use the Name of Jesus the way He intended if you're not yielded to God in every area of your life. An example is if you're operating in strife, unforgiveness, hate, or fear. The Bible has much to say about these things.

"For where envying and strife is, there is confusion and every evil work."
(James 3:16, KJV 1900)

"Now the works of the flesh are evident, which are: adultery, fornication, uncleanness, lewdness, idolatry, sorcery, hatred, contentions, jealousies, outbursts of wrath, selfish ambitions, dissensions, heresies, envy, murders, drunkenness, revelries, and the like; of which I tell you beforehand, just as I also told you in time past, that those

who practice such things will not inherit the kingdom of God."
(Galatians 5:19–21, NKJV)

"But if ye forgive not men their trespasses, neither will your Father forgive your trespasses."
(Matthew 6:15, KJV 1900)

This is not an exhaustive list, by any means. These are only a few of the verses on these subjects, so I'd encourage you to study them out for yourself, because there isn't enough space in this book to address all of them. Any of these "works of the flesh" can kill your faith quickly, rendering you ineffective in the Kingdom of God, so you must avoid them at all costs.

I've previously said that there's a price to pay for the privilege of operating in the Kingdom of God. The cost is time spent reading the Bible, fellowshipping with the Lord, and keeping yourself free from sin. When people come to me complaining that the promises in the Bible don't work for them, a closer inspection reveals that they have one or more of these sins operating in their lives. And the Bible is clear that we are not to give place to the devil.

"Neither give place to the devil."
(Ephesians 4:27, KJV 1900)

Believers give place to the devil all the time, as evidenced by their thoughts, feelings, emotions, and actions. How can they possibly operate in the full authority of the Kingdom of God when they align themselves with the kingdom of darkness?

I'd like to emphasize that you can only use the authority granted to you in the Bible. Anything outside of that is operating in presumption, and grave consequences can result. Here's an example. I've known people who, full of themselves, decide to take authority over another person's spouse. They decide the spouse should be theirs instead. Or they do this with other people's belongings. This is selfish and covetous, and the authority granted to the believer does not cover this situation.

Here's another example. You don't have the authority to override someone else's will. I once encountered someone who complained about demonic manifestations in his home. I offered to go to his house to take care of it, but he said that he allowed the entities to be there. This had to do with his religious beliefs. As much as I wanted to help him, I couldn't. He was unwilling to do anything about the situation even though he complained about it. Those entities could have lashed out at me if I had attempted to take authority over them. They would have had the right to do it because I was exceeding my authority and operating in presumption, and they would have known that.

Now, let me make a qualifying statement here. If the Lord had specifically given me instructions to take authority over them, then I would have been within my authority. I couldn't take action since He didn't. Be very careful about using your authority on other people if they are not willing and if the Lord has not given you specific instructions regarding that situation. And never use your authority for selfish gain.

There's so much to write on this topic, but this chapter is just an overview of the subject. If you'd like to study this further on your own, I recommend reading through the Books of Matthew, Mark, Luke, John, and Acts so you can see exactly how Jesus and His apostles used their authority. That's the authority that has been granted to you, so see for yourself how they did it. He also gave you power over the enemy (Luke 10:19), so learn about your authority and start using it to overcome the negative circumstances in your life. You don't have to be a victim any longer.

Chapter Four: Prayer

PRAYER IS ONE OF THE MOST IMPORTANT PRINCIPLES YOU can learn, and learning how to do it is the focus of this chapter.

Let's start off with the first question I'm asked by new believers: "What is prayer?" Simply put, it is communicating and fellowshipping with God. Many theologians will provide deeply spiritual answers, but it all boils down to talking to your Heavenly Father. We are His children, so we should be able to talk to Him about anything. You can talk to Him about what you wear to work, what you eat, or anything else you have on your mind. I've heard preachers say that God doesn't have time to deal with such small-time stuff, but that's absurd, because God isn't bound by time. So, talk to Him about anything. He's the ultimate Father, so He cares about the things that affect your life.

All prayer is communicating with God, and there are several types of prayer, each with its own purpose. For example, there's the prayer of intercession that we use to pray on behalf of someone else. There's also the prayer of dedication and consecration that we use to dedicate our life wholly to God and submit our will to His. There are several more besides these, but this chapter focuses on the prayer of petition that we use to bring our needs before the Father.

This is the type of prayer with which believers express the most frustration. Their prayers aren't being answered and they don't know why. It's usually because they aren't praying according to Biblical principles. I don't want to reduce prayer to a recipe or a set of keys or steps, but there are some critical principles to follow to ensure your prayers are answered. Many Christians, especially new believers, don't know how to begin unless they are given a list of steps to work with, so that's why I will provide some steps here.

Bearing that in mind, let's begin with the basic steps and then we'll go into detail.

- Step 1: Repent of any unforgiveness BEFORE you pray.
- Step 2: Determine what you want to receive from God.
- Step 3: Find the Scriptures that promise you what you're asking for.
- Step 4: Ask God for what you want.
- Step 5: Believe you receive when you pray.
- Step 6: Take action on what you believe, because faith without works is dead.
- Step 7: Continue to stand firm in the belief that you received what you asked for when you prayed.

Step 1: Repent of any unforgiveness BEFORE you pray. In all my years of teaching and training on prayer, I'd have to say that this is the biggest issue for most Christians and is also the reason their prayers are not answered.

Why am I listing this step first? Because if you refuse to forgive others their offenses, God will not forgive yours. You should not expect to have your prayers answered if you're harboring unforgiveness toward someone. Let's look at some key Scriptures that will make this point.

"And when ye stand praying, forgive, if ye have ought against any: that your Father also which is in heaven may forgive you your trespasses. But if ye do not forgive, neither will your Father which is in heaven forgive your trespasses."
(Mark 11:25–26, KJV 1900)

"For if you forgive people their sins, your heavenly Father will also forgive you. But if you do not forgive people, neither will your Father forgive your sins."
(Matthew 6:14–15, LEB)

"Judge not, and you shall not be judged. Condemn not, and you shall not be condemned. Forgive, and you will be forgiven."
(Luke 6:37, NKJV)

I've lost count of the number of times someone argued with me about forgiveness. They still think they have the right not to forgive someone, even though I provide several verses of Scripture, a few of which I just listed. It's usually because they thought the particular sin the person committed against them was big enough to warrant an exception.

"But you don't know what they did to me," they say.

"They don't deserve my forgiveness because they haven't apologized to me yet."

"God understands how I feel."

And so on.

These are very dangerous arguments to make. God's Word does NOT say to forgive when you feel like it or only when the sin is small enough to warrant it. It says to forgive regardless of the offense and regardless of its size. There are no exceptions.

Here's another thing that happens. People will say that harboring a grudge is not the same as not forgiving someone. Who do you think you're kidding with this ridiculous argument?

Read the Parable of the Unforgiving Servant in Matthew 18:21-35 if you still doubt what I'm saying.

> *"Then came Peter to him, and said, Lord, how oft shall my brother sin against me, and I forgive him? till seven times? Jesus saith unto him, I say not unto thee, Until seven times: but, Until seventy times seven. Therefore is the kingdom of heaven likened unto a certain king, which would take account of his servants. And when he had begun to reckon, one was brought unto him, which owed him ten thousand talents. But forasmuch as he had not to pay, his lord commanded him to be sold, and his wife, and children, and all that he had, and payment to be made. The servant therefore fell down, and worshipped him, saying, Lord, have patience with me, and I will pay thee all. Then the lord of that servant was moved with compassion, and loosed him, and forgave him the debt. But the same servant went out, and found one of his fellowservants, which owed him an hundred pence: and he laid hands on him, and took him by the throat, saying, Pay me that thou owest.*

And his fellowservant fell down at his feet, and besought him, saying, Have patience with me, and I will pay thee all. And he would not: but went and cast him into prison, till he should pay the debt. So when his fellowservants saw what was done, they were very sorry, and came and told unto their lord all that was done. Then his lord, after that he had called him, said unto him, O thou wicked servant, I forgave thee all that debt, because thou desiredst me: Shouldest not thou also have had compassion on thy fellowservant, even as I had pity on thee? And his lord was wroth, and delivered him to the tormentors, till he should pay all that was due unto him. So likewise shall my heavenly Father do also unto you, if ye from your hearts forgive not every one his brother their trespasses."

(Matthew 18:21–35, KJV 1900)

Some people will argue that this parable relates specifically to money but that's not the case. Focus on verse 35, which uses the word 'trespasses'. Synonyms for this word include mistake, fault, error, or wrongdoing, and do not relate to money only.

"So likewise shall my heavenly Father do also unto you, if ye from your hearts forgive not every one his brother their trespasses."

(Matthew 18:35, KJV 1900)

Read these verses again and again. It's important to understand that forgiveness is not an option. It's a God-given directive. Forgiveness does not mean the person you forgive is getting away with anything. However, when you forgive, it puts the matter in the hands of the Judge of All so He can handle it His way. It is not up to us to act as judge and jury in a matter.

Once you have forgiven those who have wronged you, you're free to move on to the next step.

Step 2: Determine what you need or want from God. As crazy as this might sound, many people I talk to who are frustrated with their prayer life can't tell me what they're praying for. They just start talking to God, but don't specifically ask for anything. Let's look at James 4:2,3 to get an idea of the problem.

"You lust and do not have. You murder and
covet and cannot obtain. You fight and war.
Yet you do not have because you do not ask.
You ask and do not receive, because you ask amiss, that
you may spend it on your pleasures."
(James 4:2–3, NKJV)

You can see from this verse that people do not receive because they do not ask. Then they ask but don't receive because they ask amiss (wrongly), which we'll focus on in the next step. Therefore, ask for something specific to ensure your prayers are answered. Be very clear about it.

Let's break this down using the example of a someone who needs a job. I need to determine the type of job, the location, the hours, the salary range, etc., before I approach God about this. It's critical that you spend time in prayer about this. You can also ask the Holy Spirit for guidance on what to ask for.

The most critical aspect of this step is to make sure that you can believe in God to provide what you're asking for. This trips people up all the time. Let me explain.

Using the example of someone who needs a new job, let's assume that I decide I want to run a Fortune 500 company. I'm working as a clerk at a convenience store, and I don't have any of the qualifications to run a Fortune 500 company, so do you think I have enough faith to believe that God will provide a position such as this? Absolutely not, yet people do this all the time. They ask for the most bizarre things. Some of it is so outlandish that nothing short of a miracle could bring it to pass. You must ensure that your faith is at an appropriate level to believe for whatever it is you're asking for before you pray.

Let me explain it this way. Everyone has been given the measure of faith (Romans 12:3), but like a muscle, we must exercise faith for it to grow. You wouldn't expect a newborn baby to lift a 100-pound weight ten minutes after being born, would you? Yet that's exactly what's happening if you work at a convenience store and decide you want to run a major corporation. There are steps to building your faith. Just as the newborn will not lift a heavy weight right away, neither will you be able to believe that God will cause you to become the CEO of a large corporation until you have built up your faith for it. Understand that getting a job running a Fortune 500 company would require a miracle if you're working as a clerk at a convenience store. You have a part to play in this equation. You must ensure that your faith can stand up to what you're asking God for. God has His part to play, but you also have yours: Make sure you can believe Him for it.

"Jesus said to him, "If you can believe, all things are possible to him who believes.""
(Mark 9:23, NKJV)

You can see from this Scripture that all things are possible to the person who believes, but you have to make sure you're believing and not wishing, because they are two entirely different things. A wish is a strong desire or hope for something, but a belief is a conviction that something is true. Wishing won't get you anything from God but believing will, so make sure you're in a state of belief about whatever it is you want from God. Let's look at two Scripture verses that make this point very clear.

"But Jesus said to him, "If you are able! All things are possible for the one who believes!""
(Mark 9:23, LEB)

"Therefore I say to you, whatever things you ask when you pray, believe that you receive them, and you will have them."
(Mark 11:24, NKJV)

Both verses of Scripture use the term 'believe' for a reason, because believing is required, not hoping or wishing.

Let's look at this situation again and see what I can believe in God to provide for. Using the same scenario as before, I am a clerk at a convenience store, but I'd like a better job with advancement opportunities. I think about it and decide that I'd like to find a job as a salesperson at one of the large department stores in town. I can *see* myself doing this. When I say that I can **see** myself with it, I mean I can envision it and I'm certain that I can believe in God for it. I can *see* it happening. It will stretch my faith to believe for that, because I've never worked as a salesperson before, but I know I can believe in God for an entry-level position at one of these stores. Now I'm ready for the next step.

Step 3: Find the Scriptures that promise you what you're asking for. You must find Scriptures that back up your request to ensure an answer to your prayer. Some people ask for the most outlandish things for which there's no Scriptural support. I know of people who expect God to meet their needs by having someone send a check to their mailboxes each month. The Word of God does not promise you this. Here are some other bizarre requests people have made.

- Praying to lose 100 pounds overnight
- Praying to marry a man who is already married
- Praying to win the lottery

You cannot pray outside the will of God and expect an answer. However, using the previous example, would I be able to find some Scriptures that promise me a job or a better job than the one I have? Absolutely. Let's go find them.

There are a few things I can do to locate the Scriptures that promise me what I want if I'm not sure where to look in the Bible. I can ask my pastor, or I can use a concordance, which is an alphabetical list of words in a text. I can also do a general Internet search if neither option is available to me at the moment. I decide to do an Internet search because I want to work on this immediately.

Let me first caution you that if you decide to use the Internet to find Scriptures, you must research for yourself whatever you find. Never take an Internet search at face value. Do the work to make sure you get it right. This would include making sure the Scripture is being used in the correct context and that it promises what you're asking for. Additionally, make sure you find more than one Scripture.

I did a general Internet search, so now I go to my browser and enter 'Scriptures about jobs'. I see many results, so now I need to filter them down and make sure they apply to my situation. I settle on the following verses after finishing my research. These will be the basis for my request.

"And that ye study to be quiet, and to do your own business, and to work with your own hands, as we commanded you;"
(1 Thessalonians 4:11, KJV 1900)

"Now such persons we command and encourage in the Lord Jesus Christ to do their work quietly and to earn their own living."
(2 Thessalonians 3:12, ESV)

"The hand of the diligent will rule,
while the slothful will be put to forced labor."
(Proverbs 12:24, ESV)

"Wealth gained by dishonesty will be diminished,
But he who gathers by labor will increase."
(Proverbs 13:11, NKJV)

"Look! I have discovered what is good and fitting: to eat and to drink and to enjoy all the fruit of the toil with which one toils under the sun during the number of the days of his life that God gives to him—for this is his lot. This indeed is a gift of God: everyone to whom God gives wealth and possessions, he also empowers him to enjoy them, to accept his lot, and to rejoice in the fruit of his toil."
(Ecclesiastes 5:18–19, LEB)

"For even when we were with you, we used to command this to you: that if anyone does not want to work, neither should he eat."
(2 Thessalonians 3:10, LEB)

Now that I've located Bible verses that support my request, I'm ready to make my official petition to God.

Step 4: Ask God for what you want. Using the previous example, I'll pray for my new job.

"Heavenly Father, in Jesus' Name, I come before You today to petition for a new job. Your Word is clear that I am to earn my living. I desire a new, better-paying job, and I'd like it to be as a salesperson at one of the major department stores in town. I want this job to have advancement opportunities.

I will listen for Your voice and will do as You say as You lead me through finding my new job. And as I look for my new job, I will continue to honor my current employer by doing my best.

Father, I know my prayers are hindered if there's unforgiveness in my heart, so I have forgiven everyone who has done me wrong. I harbor no unforgiveness toward anyone.

I thank You for my new job, and I believe I have received what I have requested from You."

I'll go into more detail about the statement "I believe I receive" in the next step. For now, it's important to mention that you can customize this prayer for any petition you want to make that aligns with the Word of God.

Another thing to keep in mind is that you must always pray in Jesus' Name. It is not scriptural to pray in God's Name, though you may hear people, including pastors, do that from time to time.

"And on that day you will ask me nothing.
Truly, truly I say to you, whatever you ask the
Father in my name, he will give you."
(John 16:23, LEB)

Step 5: Believe you receive when you pray. This step is often the hardest to understand, yet it's the most important. This is where faith comes in. It's about having confidence in the Word of God.

Your prayer will be answered if you pray according to God's will (1 John 5:14-15).

"And this is the confidence that we have in him, that, if we
ask any thing according to his will, he heareth us: And if
we know that he hear us, whatsoever we ask, we know that

we have the petitions that we desired of him."
(1 John 5:14–15, KJV 1900)

That's why it's so important to find Scriptures that promise you what you're asking for, because now you know you're asking according to His will. You aren't guessing. There can be a time span between making the petition and having it materialize, but that doesn't change the fact that you have it. You must **believe** that you received when you prayed, and now you stand on the promises of God and let them do their work.

Step 6: You must take action on what you believe, because faith without works is dead. I must take action by putting in job applications if I believe I have received a new job. In this case, I prayed and believed God for a sales job at one of the major department stores in town. I submit applications to the major department stores to put my faith into action. You must do everything you know to do, but always be led by the Holy Spirit. He may lead you to do something strange, but you must obey. I'll give you an example from my life.

Many years ago, the company where I worked as an accountant was acquired. The acquiror offered me a job, but the Holy Spirit told me to take my severance package and leave. I was then out of a job. I was scared, because this was during a very difficult economic time. Jobs were scarce. People were being laid off by the thousands, and houses were being repossessed at an unprecedented rate. This was a time of famine.

As I petitioned God for another job, He stopped me and said, "I already have something for you." And that's all He said.

I figured that I'd be out of a job for perhaps two weeks or maybe even a month, but I panicked after a couple of months went by. I submitted my resume to recruiters, but after I did that, it didn't feel right. I knew I wasn't doing what God wanted, so I withdrew my resume.

A few more months went by, and I wondered if I'd really heard His voice. As I prayed again, the Lord said, "I already have something for you."

This was a time of famine, as I said earlier. It was complete madness for me not to look for work. I knew I'd heard the voice of the Holy Spirit, but I still had to deal with a lot of anxiety. Let no one tell you that obeying the voice of the Holy Spirit is easy. It isn't. Speaking for myself, I wanted to take action and look for a new job, so it was painful to be told not to. It was going against conventional wisdom.

Faith without works is dead, so I had to ask myself how much I trusted God. I wanted to look for work, but I believed I had heard His voice when He said not to. So, there I sat, day after day, for several months.

I panicked again as the months passed, because the balance of my savings account was going down. However, when I prayed, the Lord said, "You will receive a call from somebody you know, and it will be somebody you haven't heard from in a while. The person will offer you a job and you are to accept. You need not worry. You will not run out of money."

Another six weeks went by, but that call finally came, and it turned out exactly as the Holy Spirit had said. I accepted the job, and I never ran out of money. In fact, my lifestyle did not change during the entire eight and a half months of unemployment.

Why am I telling you all of this? Because you need to know that there will be times when the Holy Spirit tells you to do something that goes against everything you know and believe. For me, it was a tremendous step of faith to not look for work when everything I knew showed that I should be. It was painful to stay at home and wait day after day for the phone to ring.

I spent a lot of time in the Word and in prayer while I was unemployed, building up my faith. As I look back, I can easily say that this was the most challenging directive the Holy Spirit has ever given me, but now I have this experience with God. I know I can trust Him. I know He will never leave me or forsake me.

You can trust God to lead you every step of the way in your life. You need to know that God takes it seriously when you make a petition to Him based on His Word. His Word is His bond. God's Word is His promise to you.

"For when God made a promise to Abraham, since he had no one greater to swear by, he swore by himself,"
(Hebrews 6:13, LEB)

"I will worship toward Your holy temple, And praise Your name For Your lovingkindness and Your truth; For You have magnified Your word above all Your name."
(Psalm 138:2, NKJV)

God has magnified His Word above even His own Name as these verses show. This is what should give you the confidence to trust Him. He won't let you down.

Step 7: Continue to stand firm in the belief that you received what you asked for when you prayed. Even if there's a gap between the time you prayed and the manifestation of that prayer, don't undo your prayer with a statement of unbelief. For example, if you prayed for a new job, but it doesn't manifest right away, then don't undo it by saying, "I don't think I'll ever find a new job." If you do that, you have just undone your prayer.

If you catch yourself speaking a statement of unbelief, repent and ask the Lord to forgive your unbelief and to render your unbelieving words null and void. Then continue to praise and thank Him for your new job.

If you struggle to stay in faith, remember that faith comes by hearing, according to Romans 10:17.

"Consequently, faith comes by hearing, and hearing through the word about Christ."
(Romans 10:17, LEB)

If you need to grow your faith in a particular area, then find resources on that topic and listen to them repeatedly until your faith increases. Remember: A baby won't be able to lift a 100-pound weight a few minutes after being born. As he grows, he will start by lifting small weights and then gradually he will be able to lift that 100-pound weight.

This is also the case with faith. You will need to develop your faith over time. Faith comes by hearing the Word of God over and over. The Word of God is food for your spirit. The more you consume, the stronger your spirit man will grow. Start by believing God for smaller things; as you gain experience, you can believe for bigger and bigger things.

However, remember that you have a part to play in this. God will do His part, but you have to do yours, so make sure you can believe in God to provide for what you're asking for. Pray and let the Holy Spirit guide you if you're not sure. Stay in faith and make sure your words align with what you're believing for. Don't undo your prayer with words of unbelief.

As you begin your adventure of faith with God, you'll see that He's faithful every time.

Chapter Five:
Promise Of Protection

IT'S SAD TO SAY, BUT MANY CHRISTIANS TODAY KNOW NOTHING about their promise of protection. They walk around afraid of the dark, afraid of financial ruin, afraid of sickness and disease, afraid of being killed in a car accident, and afraid of just about everything.

Yet Jesus paid a high price for us to live free from fear. In fact, Jesus told us He did not give us the spirit of fear (2 Timothy 1:7). If you live with fear, it's not from your Heavenly Father, it's from the enemy.

Jesus purchased our freedom from hell when we die when He died on the cross, but He also purchased many other things, one of which is freedom from fear. We don't have to live with it any longer. Fear has no right to hold us in bondage. However, if you don't know the protection that's available to you, that's essentially the same as not having it at all. What good is a weapon if you don't know you have it?

I automatically think of Psalm 91 when I think of protection. I refer to it as the 'Circle of Protection' or the 'Wall of Protection', but whatever you want to call it, it's your covenant of protection as a believer. This protection, while available to all believers, doesn't come automatically. We must appropriate it. What do I mean by that? Let's look at what Psalm 91 tells us, starting with verses 1 and 2.

"He that dwelleth in the secret place of the most
High Shall abide under the shadow of the Almighty.
I will say of the LORD, He is my refuge and my fortress:
My God; in him will I trust."
(Psalm 91:1–2, KJV 1900, emphasis added)

The person who trusts in the Lord isn't afraid to say so. He trusts in the Lord with all his might. In saying that you trust in the Lord, you say that no matter what happens, you trust Him with your life. You know He will come through, regardless of what comes against you.

Many people reading this will ask why so many Christians die prematurely in car wrecks, acts of nature, and so forth, if Psalm 91 is true? Would you like the honest answer? Because their wall of protection wasn't in place. This isn't a condemnation. We, as believers, often settle for much less than what our Heavenly Father offers. I could share story after story of people who appropriated the 91st Psalm for themselves in times of danger and came out unscathed. These people believed, really believed, that the Lord would protect them in times of trouble.

"Surely he shall deliver thee from the snare of the fowler,
And from the noisome pestilence. He shall cover thee with
his feathers, And under his wings shalt thou trust: His
truth shall be thy shield and buckler."
(Psalm 91:3–4, KJV 1900)

Verses 3 and 4 promise us He will deliver us from those who wish to ensnare us and from every deadly pestilence or plague. He covers us with His feathers just like a mother hen. He shields us from anything that can hurt us.

"Thou shalt not be afraid for the terror by night; Nor for the arrow that flieth by day; Nor for the pestilence that walketh in darkness; Nor for the destruction that wasteth at noonday. A thousand shall fall at thy side, And ten thousand at thy right hand; But it shall not come nigh thee. Only with thine eyes shalt thou behold And see the reward of the wicked."
(Psalm 91:5–8, KJV 1900)

We don't have to be afraid of anything: neither terror, destruction, nor anything else. Nothing can touch us if we trust Him with our well-being. It won't come near us even if we see a thousand fall by our sides or ten thousand at our right hand. It will hit the Wall of Protection. It doesn't matter what tries to come against us. Nothing on this planet can get past that Wall if we trust in the Lord to protect us. No matter how close it gets, it cannot touch us, and we won't take part in it, even if we see the reward of those who are wicked and unrighteous.

"Because thou hast made the LORD, which is my refuge, Even the most High, thy habitation; There shall no evil befall thee, Neither shall any plague come nigh thy dwelling."
(Psalm 91:9–10, KJV 1900)

If you have made the Lord your refuge, meaning that you trust in Him to protect you, and if you trust Him to lead and guide you, then no evil will happen to you. No plagues can come near your house or your family.

Let's dig into these verses a little more before we move on. "If you have made the Lord your refuge" means that if you have made the conscious decision to make Him your refuge, then the rest of the verse applies to you. Therefore, Psalm 91 doesn't always apply to everyone. Remember, we must appropriate these promises; they don't come automatically.

"For he shall give his angels charge over thee, To keep thee in all thy ways. They shall bear thee up in their hands, Lest thou dash thy foot against a stone."
(Psalm 91:11–12, KJV 1900)

Many Christians do not believe in the protection of angels, but it isn't wise to discount it. Every believer has guardian angels that keep charge over them. They're responsible for your well-being, but they only hearken to the Word of God. You can tie their hands if you're speaking things contrary to the Word. They have to sit on the sidelines and watch negative things happen to you because you've bound them. Their purpose is to minister to believers, but they respond only to the Word.

"Are they not all ministering spirits, sent forth to minister for them who shall be heirs of salvation?"
(Hebrews 1:14, KJV 1900)

"Bless the Lord, ye his angels, That excel in strength, that do his commandments, Hearkening unto the voice of his word."
(Psalm 103:20, KJV 1900)

If you're in the middle of a dangerous situation and scream, "Oh no, I think I'm going to die!", then you have overridden your protective covering. Think I'm joking? Look at the verse below and tell me if it means anything other than what it says.

"Death and life are in the power of the tongue, and those who love her will eat of her fruit."
(Proverbs 18:21, LEB)

You cannot speak words of death for the protective wall to remain around you. Your words govern whether you enjoy protection.

> *"Thou shalt tread upon the lion and adder: The young lion and the dragon shalt thou trample under feet. Because he hath set his love upon me, therefore will I deliver him: I will set him on high, because he hath known my name.* ***He shall call upon me, and I will answer him****: I will be with him in trouble; I will deliver him, and honour him. With long life will I satisfy him, And shew him my salvation."*
> (Psalm 91:13–16, KJV 1900, emphasis added)

We are to call on the Lord in times of trouble, and He promises to deliver us. This is a promise. It's important that we get this down into our spirits because it's a sure thing that we'll need it at some point. For that reason, I recommend memorizing Psalm 91 in its entirety. That way, it's available to you when you need it. Remember, it is not possible for a believer to be in fear and faith at the same time, so we need to make sure that we don't allow fear into our lives.

Psalm 91 requires that you take up residence under God's protection. How do you do that? Verse 2 declares, 'I will say of the Lord that He is my refuge and fortress.' It comes from your words and your belief.

Understanding your promise of protection is important for the days in which we live. It's not an exaggeration to say that things keep getting darker and darker every day, but we don't have to surrender to the negativity. We can rise above it by trusting the Lord.

Let's look at more verses that speak of God's protection.

> *"Whoever listens to me will dwell in security and rest securely from dread and disaster."*
> (Proverbs 1:33, LEB)

> *"There shall no evil happen to the just: But the wicked shall be filled with mischief."*
> (Proverbs 12:21, KJV 1900)

"A tower of strength is the name of Yahweh; into him the righteous will run and be safe."
(Proverbs 18:10, LEB)

"No weapon formed against you shall prosper, And every tongue which rises against you in judgment You shall condemn. This is the heritage of the servants of the LORD, And their righteousness is from Me," Says the LORD."
(Isaiah 54:17, NKJV)

"The Lord will keep you from all evil; he will keep your life. The Lord will keep your going out and your coming in from this time forth and forevermore."
(Psalm 121:7–8, ESV)

Remember that you can override your covenant of protection with the words of your mouth. Life and death are in the power of the tongue, so choose wisely what comes out of your mouth. Read and meditate on verses about the subject to build faith for protection. The ones I've provided throughout this chapter are just a few, but there are more verses throughout the Bible, so I encourage you to do your own study.

We will look at authentic examples of supernatural protection to have a proper understanding of how powerful the protection of God really is. The first example is Daniel and the lions' den, recorded in Daniel 6.

King Darius had set one hundred and twenty officials over his kingdom, but he preferred Daniel over all of them and thought to make him the top official. The jealous officials tried to find fault with Daniel but couldn't, so they gathered together and devised a plan. They asked the king to issue a decree that any man who made a petition of any god or man besides the king for thirty days would be thrown into the den of lions. They convinced the king to issue the decree, which no one could alter.

Daniel knew about the decree, yet he did not change his habit of praying to God three times a day. He did it out in the open where everyone could see, including the officials. They tattled to the king as soon as they caught him violating the decree. This king thought highly of Daniel and sought a way to deliver him, but the law of the Medes and Persians could not be altered once the king signed the decree. Thus, the king had no choice in this matter: He had to consign Daniel to the lions' den. They threw him into the den, and the king would spend a sleepless night worrying about him.

The king rushed to the den the following morning and called for Daniel. He asked if Daniel's God had saved him from the hungry lions, and Daniel replied, "My God has sent His angel to shut the mouth of the lions so they could not hurt me." King Darius, angered at those who had accused Daniel, had them all rounded up and thrown into the den, together with their families.

There's an important truth to catch here. God commands His children to have no other gods before Him, so Daniel knew he couldn't honor King Darius' decree. The lions couldn't harm him because he did the right thing, and because he trusted his God, God sent angels to protect him from the lions.

Daniel had a choice: He could yield to fear, which is what many people would have done, but he didn't. He trusted his God, and God delivered him. Proverbs 29:25 tells us that the Lord will keep safe those who trust in Him.

Let's look next at the story in Daniel 3 of the three Hebrew boys, Shadrach, Meshach, and Abednego. King Nebuchadnezzar had made an image of gold and commanded that all people were to bow down and worship it when they heard music. They would toss anyone who refused that command into a fiery furnace.

The three Hebrew boys did not bow down, and the Chaldeans told the king about it. The king asked if the charges were true when the boys were brought before him. He even gave them one last chance to prove their allegiance, but they still refused. The king became so enraged that he ordered the furnace heated seven times hotter than normal. The furnace was so hot that it killed the men who went near it.

Into the fire the three men went. However, the king then noticed that there were four men walking around in the flames, and the fourth was like the Son of God. He called to Shadrach, Meshach, and Abednego to come out of the furnace, and they did. Those standing around noticed that it had not singed a hair on their head. King Nebuchadnezzar suddenly realized that their God had sent His angels to save them. The king commanded that nobody should speak against their God from that point forward, because only their God could save this way.

Did you ever notice that God didn't stop Daniel from getting thrown into the lions' den, or Shadrach, Meshach, and Abednego from being tossed into the fiery furnace? Many people think that God's protection means they will never get tossed into the equivalent of a lions' den or a fiery furnace, but that thinking misses the point. You may indeed be tossed into the proverbial lions' den, but trusting in God means you know that He's there with you every step of the way.

There are many other examples of God's supernatural protection in the Bible. Acts 12:3-11 tells of Peter being broken out of jail by an angel. Acts 16:25-27 also provides the account of Paul and Silas being broken out of jail by an angel.

God can protect His children when they trust in Him, but the key here is trust. Many people say they trust God, but their words say otherwise. Doubt will leave you open to the plans and purposes of the enemy. I encourage you to read this chapter over and over until you believe in your heart that God will come through for you as well. He is a good God and loves us more than we could ever imagine. His protection is available to every believer, but it requires trust - trust that He will never leave us nor forsake us.

Chapter Six: What About The Tithe?

WHAT IS THE TITHE? MANY HEAR THIS WORD BANDIED ABOUT but don't know what it means. Tithe means the tenth part, or ten percent. The action of tithing means to give a tenth of your income. Tithing occurred in the Old Testament and New Testament, yet there remains a debate about whether God requires Christians to tithe today. I'd like you to read a few verses of Scripture on the subject before we dive into a discussion about tithing.

"And blessed be the most high God, which hath delivered thine enemies into thy hand. And he gave him ***tithes*** *of all."*
(Genesis 14:20, KJV 1900, emphasis added)

"To whom also Abraham gave a ***tenth part*** *of all; first being by interpretation King of righteousness, and after that also King of Salem, which is, King of peace;"*
(Hebrews 7:2, KJV 1900, emphasis added)

"Will a man rob God? Yet ye have robbed me. But ye say, Wherein have we robbed thee? In ***tithes*** *and offerings."*
(Malachi 3:8, KJV 1900, emphasis added)

"And here men that die receive ***tithes****; but there he receiveth them, of whom it is witnessed that he liveth."*
(Hebrews 7:8, KJV 1900, emphasis added)

Christians accuse pastors who bring up the subject of tithing of trying to get their money. Nobody gets to accuse me of that, because I'm not a pastor, don't operate a church, and don't accept tithes and offerings on behalf of church members. Therefore, I can say this without somebody accusing me of bilking people out of their hard-earned money. Tithe! Just as tithing was in effect before the Law of Moses and was in effect after Jesus died, so it is today, regardless of what anyone else has told you. We'll get into that deeper in this chapter, but decide right now to stop robbing God (Malachi 3:8-10).

Anyone who has experienced hurt by pastors who just wanted your money need to get over it and leave that in the past. Forgive them and move forward. Today is a new day. Take responsibility for going before God to find out where you should tithe. Don't just give into any offering bucket that's placed in front of you, and don't give just because someone tells you they need the money. The tithe is a holy thing and must be treated with great respect. The tithe also reflects the condition of your heart, so it's a very serious matter.

For the record, tithing predates the Law and is also part of the New Covenant. Many people like to say that tithing isn't for today. They say that it went into effect as part of the Law and went away with the death of Jesus on the cross. They couldn't be more wrong. If this statement makes you mad, give me a few minutes of your time before you close this book and throw it away, thinking that I'm some sort of heretic. I've worked with well-meaning Christian people over the years whose lives were a mess.

They didn't realize they were operating under a curse. Once they got this one thing straightened out, things got better.

Let's first deal with the fact that tithing existed before the Law of Moses. Let's look at Genesis 14:18-20 together from the King James version.

"And Melchizedek king of Salem brought forth bread and wine: and he was the priest of the most high God. And he blessed him, and said, Blessed be Abram of the most high God, possessor of heaven and earth: And blessed be the most high God, which hath delivered thine enemies into thy hand. And he gave him tithes of all."
(Genesis 14:18–20, KJV 1900)

Are there other examples of tithing besides this one involving Abram? Yes. Let's read Genesis 28:20-22.

"And Jacob vowed a vow, saying, 'If God will be with me, and will keep me in this way that I go, and will give me bread to eat, and raiment to put on, So that I come again to my father's house in peace; then shall the LORD be my God: And this stone, which I have set for a pillar, shall be God's house: and of all that thou shalt give me ***I will surely give the tenth unto thee.****'"*
(Genesis 28:20–22, KJV 1900, emphasis added)

We also find verses related to tithing in the New Testament. One such verse is in Hebrews 7:8.

"Here mortal men receive tithes, but there he receives them, of whom it is witnessed that he lives."
(Hebrews 7:8, NKJV)

The authorship of Hebrews remains in dispute, yet many scholars attribute it to the Apostle Paul. Regardless of who wrote it, we find that tithing existed after the death of our Lord and Savior, Jesus Christ.

We can find other Scriptures on tithing in Matthew 23:23 and Luke 11:42. I encourage you to read them for yourself.

Many people have asked why God instituted tithing. Rather than guess, let's let the Bible speak for itself. We find the answer in Malachi 3:10.

"'Bring all the tithes into the storehouse,
That there may be food in My house, And try Me now in
this,' Says the LORD of hosts, 'If I will not open for you the
windows of heaven And pour out for you such blessing
That there will not be room enough to receive it.'"
(Malachi 3:10, NKJV)

The reason is that God wanted there to be food in His house. We find additional clarity when we read 2 Chronicles 31:4-5.

"Moreover he commanded the people who dwelt in Jerusalem to contribute support for the priests and the Levites, ***that they might devote themselves to the Law of the LORD.*** *As soon as the commandment was circulated, the children of Israel brought in abundance the firstfruits of grain and wine, oil and honey, and of all the produce of the field; and they brought in abundantly the tithe of everything."*
(2 Chronicles 31:4–5, NKJV, emphasis added)

The tithe sustained the priests and Levites so they could focus on the Law of the Lord. They didn't have to go out and get a second job, in other words. That would be the case now if that was the case then. Pastors and teachers would have to get a second job to meet the church expenses if church members didn't tithe. Think about it. God wanted His priests and Levites sustained back then, so wouldn't He also want that for those He has called to the ministry now? Tithing is necessary to ensure that His churches can function. That's what it means to have meat in His house. How do you expect the churches to function without money? It needs to come from somewhere, so God established the tithe. However, this isn't the only reason for the tithe. We find in Deuteronomy 14:22-23 that tithing has the additional purpose of teaching us to revere the Lord our God. It helps us to keep money in its proper place. We'll handle money properly and not let the love of money take over if we remember the Lord our God.

One of the first things to get straight in your mind as we continue our discussion on tithing is the fact that God comes first, not your bills. Lots of people claim they can't tithe, but the truth is they *can't* afford not to tithe. That tithe ties you to the covenant. It's not comfortable tithing when you're facing a mountain of debt and unpaid bills, but that tenth belongs to God regardless of what else is going on in our lives. Doing something else with it ultimately robs God and places you under the curse spoken of in Malachi.

The second thing to get straight is that tithe means "tenth." It doesn't mean five percent, nor does it mean fifteen percent. It means one tenth. Period. You haven't tithed if you give less than ten percent. When you hear someone say that they tithe fifteen percent, what they mean is that they tithe the tenth, or ten percent, and then give a five percent offering. The tithe means nothing other than ten percent.

The third thing to understand is that we calculate the tithe on the gross, not the net. Many preachers say it is perfectly okay to tithe off the net, meaning after taxes are taken out, but that's not correct. We must take the tithe from the first fruits of our labor, and taxes are not part of that equation. Therefore, you must always tithe on the full amount, the gross.

I'll discuss offerings in a separate chapter, but I want to explain right now that you can't give an offering if you haven't first tithed. You're required to return to God what's His before you can give to Him what's yours. Tithing and giving offerings will bring a blessing into your life unmatched by anything the secular world can offer if you do it correctly. I know it for a fact because I've tithed and given offerings for decades, and I can tell you that financial situations that negatively affect non-tithers don't affect me. They can't, because all that I have is under His protection. I'll share some stories related to my own financial situations that might just make the hair on your head stand up straight. And if you remain unconvinced that tithing is for you after reading them, then you should close this book now and read no further. Throw it away and go back to whatever you were doing before you picked it up, because you can do everything else in this book and still fail if you don't tithe. That's how important it is.

I mentioned earlier that many preachers and teachers are afraid to teach about the tithe these days because people will accuse them of only wanting their money. However, since I don't receive tithes, I can teach it to you without that fear, because you can't accuse me of taking your money. I'm not even going to recommend some wonderful churches where you can tithe. That's between you and God. However, you will understand about the tithe before this chapter is over.

Why are people strongly opposed to the tithe today? The answer is that people don't want to part with their money, but that's flawed thinking, because everything belongs to God: We are merely stewards of what God entrusts to us. Stated more bluntly, the entire 100% is His. All He's asking us to do is willingly return to Him ten percent, and then He blesses and covers the remaining 90% over which He gives you stewardship. I'd rather have 90% that's blessed than 100% that's cursed. Therefore, if you love your money so much that you won't return to God what's His anyway, then you'll remain under a curse. Will you go to heaven? Yes, but your time here will be without the benefit of His protection over your finances. You have one other thing to deal with if you love your money: 1 Timothy 6:10, which tells us that the love of money is the root of all evil. It further states that coveting money causes people to stray from the faith, and they end up piercing themselves through with sorrows. Let's look at it closely. It says that they pierce themselves through, not their pastor, not their families, and not their friends. They do it to themselves.

"For the love of money is a root of all kinds of evil, for which some have strayed from the faith in their greediness, and ***pierced themselves*** *through with many sorrows."*
(1 Timothy 6:10, NKJV, emphasis added)

Read this verse carefully so you fully understand. Money isn't evil, but the love of it is. How do I know that money isn't evil? Let's look at the following verses for an idea of God's heart on the matter. Let's start with Deuteronomy 8:18, which says:

"But thou shalt remember the Lord thy God: for it is he that giveth thee power to get wealth, that he may establish his covenant which he sware unto thy fathers, as it is this day."
(Deuteronomy 8:18, KJV 1900)

Would God confirm His covenant with wealth if money was evil? Would He have made Abram rich? Not just rich, but very rich? God would be unrighteous for making Abraham rich if He opposed money. Then there's David, who was also wealthy. The Bible specifically states that he was a man after God's own heart. David was guilty of sin if having wealth is bad. Let's not forget Solomon: He was also rich. Thus, wealth isn't bad; when used properly, it advances God's kingdom on the earth. It's a demonstration of God's love toward His people. Poverty is under the curse (Deuteronomy 28:15-19), so prosperity would be under the blessing (Deuteronomy 28:1-14).

People who say having wealth is sinful are showing an ignorance of God's Word. Did you know that wealth and prosperity are mentioned throughout the Bible? If not, get out your Bible and read through it from start to finish. You'll see it for yourself, and when you do, you can stop thinking that being rich is bad. Being rich isn't the problem. The problem is how you act when you have received wealth. Would you be willing to give to the causes God lays on your heart? Would you trust in your wealth instead of trusting God to be your Source? He must be your everything. Your heart must be fully committed to Him; otherwise, you risk loving money, and that is a sin.

Back to the matter of tithing, I'll tell you how important it is. God promises to rebuke the devourer for your sake when you tithe. Do you have any idea what a big deal that is? As I mentioned earlier, I'd rather have 90% blessed than 100% that's cursed. I've never been without money when I needed it because of God rebuking the devourer for me. I've never been without a job when I needed it. I've never gone with bills unpaid from the time I began to tithe.

And I want to emphasize something: I'm not a preacher or pastor, so you can't tell me it's only for them. I have been under the protection the tithe affords me for a long time. I was obedient to what the Word says, and I have never been without the things I needed. I didn't start out with a bunch of money left over. I got by, but as time passed, my finances increased to where God's promise was clear in my life, the promise in which He pours out a blessing that runs over. In fact, I have more than enough, so I can give to the causes that God lays on my heart. I'm addicted to this way of living and will never go back.

Look at Proverbs 3:9-10 if you still think tithing isn't for you. These verses specifically instruct us to honor the Lord with our possessions. Other versions used the word "wealth." It says that you should honor the Lord with the first fruits of all your increase. What do you think the first fruits are? In many dictionaries, it means the first, the best, or the chief part thereof. Verse 10 of the same chapter explains the benefit of honoring the Lord this way. It says that your barns and storehouses will be filled with plenty. In today's vernacular, this would be your checking, savings, and investment accounts.

Tithing is the one area in which God challenges us to test Him. Let's look at what He said:

"Bring the full tithe into the storehouse,
that there may be food in my house. And thereby put
me to the test, says the LORD of hosts, if I will not open
the windows of heaven for you and pour down for you a
blessing until there is no more need."
(Malachi 3:10, ESV, emphasis added)

I'd challenge you to give God a chance to prove to you that tithing works. What do you have to lose?

Before we move on, I'd like to address a question I receive often, and it is how Malachi 3:10 is translated in the King James Version. Let's look at it together.

"Bring ye all the tithes into the storehouse,
That there may be meat in mine house, And prove me now
herewith, saith the LORD of hosts, If I will not open you
the windows of heaven, And pour you out a blessing, that
there shall not be room enough to receive it."
(Malachi 3:10, KJV 1900)

The main objection people have is to the statement "there shall not be enough room to receive it." Let's be honest: There's no such thing as not having enough room to receive. We can always make room for more. People question the integrity of God's Word on tithing because of that statement, but let me put your mind at ease. The King James Version isn't the most accurate translation of this verse. The King James Version of this verse includes many italicized words if you look at it closely. That means those words were not in the original manuscript. The translators added them to enhance clarity, but I don't think they were successful in this case. I believe the English Standard Version says it best.

"Bring the full tithe into the storehouse,
that there may be food in my house. And thereby put
me to the test, says the LORD of hosts, if I will not open
the windows of heaven for you and pour down for you a
blessing until there is no more need."
(Malachi 3:10, ESV)

This means that if you tithe, then God will open the windows of heaven and pour out a blessing so that you won't have any more need. This doesn't mean you won't have any more wants, but it means all your needs will be met. You can see the real promise being made if you remove all the extra words the translators added. I and countless others can attest to the truth of this verse.

The first question people ask when they decide to tithe is how it should be done. The important part about tithing is that you must tithe in faith and your motives must be pure. Yes, you can tithe out of duty, but God loves a cheerful giver (2 Corinthians 9:6-7). We should do it from a heart of love toward God. And since God doesn't reach down from heaven to accept your tithe, you would need to give to the church or ministry that feeds you spiritually.

Tithing isn't a ritual. You should tithe with purpose, not just to get that money into the offering bucket as quickly as possible so you can check off that task for the day. It's worth saying again: God loves a cheerful, purposeful giver. To do that, go before God to see where He wants that money to go. It's His, so let Him decide.

Tithe with faith and love. The tithe is to be done as an act of worship. It's a precious thing before God. If you have known sin in your life, repent of it and then bring the tithe. Known sin would also include unforgiveness you might harbor toward someone. Many people think it's okay to harbor unforgiveness toward others, but that's a dangerous stance to take. I address forgiveness in another chapter, so I won't belabor it here. You just need to know that failing to forgive others is a sin. Simple as that. So, get it all taken care of before tithing the tithe.

We are to bring the tithe because we love God, not because it's an obligation. Keep in mind that our motives are part of this equation. Read the entirety of Deuteronomy 26, which provides an outline for the act of tithing. You don't have to speak those verses word for word, but use it as an outline. An example of a prayer you can pray over your tithe is:

"Heavenly Father, I profess this day that I have come into the inheritance which You have sworn to give me. I am in the land which You have provided for me in Jesus Christ, the kingdom of Almighty God. I was a sinner serving Satan; he was my god. But I called upon the name of Jesus and You heard my cry and delivered me from the power of darkness and translated me into the kingdom of Your dear Son.

Jesus, as my Lord and High Priest, I bring the first fruits of my income to you, that You may worship the Lord my God with them. Father, I rejoice in all the good which You have given to me and my household. I have heard Your voice and have done according to all that You have commanded me.

Now Father, look down from Your holy habitation from heaven and bless me as You have said in Your Word. I believe that I now receive Your blessing according to Your Word. This is my confession of faith, in Jesus' name. Amen.

You should never toss a check carelessly into an offering bucket just to meet the tithing requirement, but neither should you treat it as a ritual. It is a time to worship God, to thank Him for all that He's done for you. I'd recommend spending time with God before you ever get to church. Make sure you can honestly say that you've heard His voice and that you've done all that He's commanded you. Go before Him if you can't say that and clean it all up so you can tithe with pure motives.

The question inevitably arises regarding what you should do if you find that you've used the tithe for something else and want to make it right before God. Let's allow the Bible to speak for itself again. We find the answer in Leviticus 27:30.

"Every tithe of the land, whether of the seed of the land or of the fruit of the trees, is the LORD's; it is holy to the LORD. If a man wishes to redeem some of his tithe, he shall add a fifth to it."
(Leviticus 27:30–31, ESV)

You owe twenty percent interest on top of the tithe if you withhold (redeem) the tithe, because there's a consequence for not tithing. Remember that the tithe is a holy thing. That doesn't mean that it's untouchable; it means that we must separate it to God. Many people try to find reasons not to tithe, but that's nothing more than an excuse to avoid returning to God what's rightfully His.

You need to start if you haven't tithed until now. This is the one subject about which God says to test Him, so test Him. Tithe. Do it according to the Word and see what happens. Search out the Scriptures for yourself. Go before God, repent for not tithing before, and commit to tithing now. Ask Him where you should give your tithe. Trust Him to lead you and guide you in this. You'll see wonderful things come out of tithing if your heart is right. Honor the Lord with your possessions, as it says in Proverbs 3:9-10, and then you'll see God become involved with your circumstances. Try it. You won't regret it.

Chapter Seven: What About The Offering?

THE PREVIOUS CHAPTER DEALT WITH THE SUBJECT OF TITHing. I'm now going to turn our attention to the offering in this chapter, because the two go hand in hand. Why do I say that? Because we find this statement in Malachi 3:8:

> "*Will a man rob God? Yet ye have robbed me. But ye say, Wherein have we robbed thee? In tithes* ***and*** *offerings.*"
> (Malachi 3:8, KJV 1900, emphasis added)

It's important to talk about the offering whenever the tithe is discussed, because you can't give an offering if you haven't first tithed. Like tithing, the offering isn't to be undertaken carelessly, because offerings can and often are rejected by God.

Let's first be clear about the fact that, while churches will accept any offering you put in the offering plate, God is under no obligation to accept it. We must give the offering under the rules He sets forth in His Word. There are keys to giving an offering that God will accept and multiply. When I say that God will accept it, I'm saying that God has bound Himself in His Word to do so. This isn't something made up by the mind of man. These are conditions God has set for Himself, so we know what will be acceptable to Him and what won't be.

Too many Christians are throwing random change into offering buckets all across America, thinking that they're doing something special for God. Many are also living in lack and want and give up on the blessings of God over their lives. This isn't by God's design. He has a simple plan in place that, if followed, will ensure you give an offering He'll accept. He's obligated Himself to multiply it back to you if He accepts it. You'll enter a place of abundance that will change your life forever if you'll take the steps to ensure you give an offering that meets the conditions God sets forth.

I'd like to emphasize that this isn't some sort of prosperity gospel teaching, nor is it the "name it and claim it" theology. This is strictly what's found in the Word of God and is available to any believer who will boldly put it into action.

First, we're going to discuss rejected offerings, because it's important to understand what not to do before we talk about what constitutes an acceptable offering. We'll look at Genesis 4:1-7 for our first example.

> *"Now Adam knew Eve his wife, and she conceived and bore Cain. And she said, 'I have given birth to a man with the help of Yahweh.' Then she bore his brother Abel. And Abel became a keeper of sheep, and Cain became a tiller of the ground. And in the course of time Cain brought an offering from the fruit of the ground to Yahweh, and Abel also brought an offering from the choicest firstlings of his flock. And Yahweh looked with favor to Abel and to his offering, but to Cain and to his offering he did not look with favor. And Cain became very angry, and his face fell. And Yahweh said to Cain, 'Why are you angry, and why is your face fallen? If you do well will I not accept you? But if you do not do well, sin is crouching at the door. And its*

desire is for you, but you must rule over it.'"
(Genesis 4:1–7, LEB)

There are several theories about what was wrong with Cain's offering, but let's not debate that here. Let's allow the Bible to speak for itself, instead. The Lord responds to Cain's anger in verse 7 by saying, "If you do well, will I not accept you?" Based on this, we can conclude that Cain knew what was right but didn't do it. He didn't follow God's prescribed method for bringing an offering. That's the crucial point to take away from this discussion.

There's another unaccepted offering in Malachi.

"'Who also among you will shut the temple doors so that you will not kindle fire in vain on my altar? I take no pleasure in you,' says Yahweh of hosts, 'and I will not accept an offering from your hand.'"
(Malachi 1:10, LEB)

There's yet another one found in 1 Samuel 15. There's a lot going on in this chapter that we can't go into here. The point is that God had told King Saul to utterly destroy the Amalekites, including their women, children, and livestock.

"Now go and smite Amalek, and utterly destroy all that they have, and spare them not; but slay both man and woman, infant and suckling, ox and sheep, camel and ass."
(1 Samuel 15:3, KJV 1900)

Yet King Saul spared Agag, along with the best of the livestock and all their valuable belongings. Everything that was despised and worthless was utterly destroyed, but he kept the best.

"But Saul and the people spared Agag, and the best of the sheep, and of the oxen, and of the fatlings, and the lambs,

and all that was good, and would not utterly destroy them: but every thing that was vile and refuse, that they destroyed utterly."
(1 Samuel 15:9, KJV 1900)

Did Saul follow God's orders? No. Thus, when the Lord spoke to Samuel about it, Samuel goes to talk to Saul. Saul explains he kept these things in order to sacrifice to Yahweh, but this was in rebellion against what God had told him to do. Thus, not only was King Saul's offering rejected, but he also lost his kingdom over his rebellion.

We find in 2 Samuel 24:18 that Gad, David's personal priest (verse 11), told David to set up an altar on the threshing floor of Araunah.

"Then Gad came to David on that same day and said to him, 'Go up and erect an altar to Yahweh at the threshing floor of Araunah the Jebusite.' So David went up according to the word of Gad, as Yahweh had commanded. Araunah looked down and saw the king and his servants coming over to him, so Araunah went out and bowed down before the king with his face to the ground. Then Araunah said, 'Why has my lord the king come to his servant?' David said, 'To buy from you the threshing floor, to build an altar to Yahweh who brought a halt to the plague on the people.' Araunah said to David, 'Let my lord the king take and offer what is good in his eyes. Look, here are the cattle for the burnt offering and the threshing sledge and the yokes of the oxen for the firewood. All of this Araunah hereby gives to the king.' Then Araunah said to the king, 'May Yahweh your God respond favorably for you.' Then the king said to Araunah, 'No, but I will certainly buy it from you for a price; I don't want to offer to Yahweh my God burnt offerings that cost me nothing.'

So David bought the threshing floor and the cattle for fifty shekels of silver. David built an altar to Yahweh there, and he offered burnt offerings and fellowship offerings. Then Yahweh responded to his prayer for the land and brought the plague to a halt from upon Israel."
(2 Samuel 24:18–25, LEB)

David offers to buy the threshing floor so that the plague can be stayed from the people, and Araunah offers it to him for free. However, David replies he won't offer something that doesn't cost him anything. The offering has to be of value, but that value isn't determined by the dollar amount. It's based on its value to the person giving it. A penny is precious if it's all you have, but if you have a lot of money, then that penny is worthless. You must look at the value to the person giving it. A few hundred thousand means nothing to you if you're a billionaire, but a few hundred thousand dollars could mean the world to someone else. Thus, it's the value to the person giving it that counts. An offering that isn't worth anything to you won't be worth anything to God, either.

Another issue that could determine whether God accepts your offering is found in Matthew 5:23-26.

"Therefore if you present your gift at the altar and there remember that your brother has something against you, leave your gift there before the altar and first go be reconciled to your brother, and then come and present your gift. Settle the case quickly with your accuser while you are with him on the way, lest your accuser hand you over to the judge, and the judge to the officer, and you be thrown into prison. Truly I say to you, you will never come out of there until you have paid back the last penny!"
(Matthew 5:23–26, LEB)

Many people ignore or completely gloss over this command, but it's critically important because we can't rebel against the Word of God and expect our offerings to be accepted. Reconcile as quickly as you can if you know your brother has an issue with you.

Another factor in an accepted offering is that it must be given willingly.

"*For if there be first a willing mind, it is accepted according to that a man hath, and not according to that he hath not.*"
(2 Corinthians 8:12, KJV 1900)

It doesn't do you any good to give when someone puts pressure on you, because then you aren't willing. The church world is rife with preachers who say you must give because of some need they have: It could be a new church building, or maybe they're trying to finance a crusade. Many preachers will play on emotions to drive up the offering. You're no longer willing if you feel coerced or guilty if you don't give.

Let's look at a few more verses.

"*Now the point is this: the one who sows sparingly will also reap sparingly, and the one who sows bountifully will also reap bountifully. Each one should give as he has decided in his heart, not reluctantly or from compulsion, for God loves a cheerful giver.*"
(2 Corinthians 9:6–7, LEB)

"*And Moses said to all the community of the Israelites, saying, 'This is the word that Yahweh has commanded, saying, Take from among you a contribution for Yahweh, anyone willing of heart, let him bring Yahweh's contribution—gold and silver and bronze,*'"
(Exodus 35:4–5, LEB)

"And they came—every man whose heart lifted him and every man whose spirit impelled him—they brought Yahweh's contribution for the work of the tent of assembly and for all its service and for the holy garments."
(Exodus 35:21, LEB)

We see in these verses that willingness was involved. You're not required to give to every preacher who asks for money. In fact, you must use discernment in giving because you could throw your money away if you do it carelessly. It's not important if the preacher accepts your offering, because churches will take whatever money ends up in the offering plates. The important question is whether God has accepted your offering, and the Word of God is clear that He loves a cheerful giver. Make sure you can be a cheerful, willing giver before you give an offering.

Another key to an accepted offering is one that is given without regard to what you don't have. Let's look at 2 Corinthians 8:12 again.

"For if there be first a willing mind, it is accepted according to that a man hath, and not according to that he hath not."
(2 Corinthians 8:12, KJV 1900)

When it comes time to consider an offering to God, many look at the remaining balance in their checkbook after they've paid all their bills and decide their giving based on that. However, that's looking at what we don't have. We're putting God into a second position when we give from whatever is left over. You'll never break out of the cycle of insufficiency if all you ever do is give what you can afford. Look at the church in Macedonia.

"We want you to know, brothers, about the grace of God that has been given among the churches of Macedonia, for in a severe test of affliction, their abundance of joy and their extreme poverty have overflowed in a wealth of generosity on their part. For they

gave according to their means, as I can testify, and beyond their means, of their own accord,"
(2 Corinthians 8:1–3, ESV)

Now let's look at the story of the widow's mite.

"And he sat down opposite the treasury and watched the people putting money into the offering box. Many rich people put in large sums. And a poor widow came and put in two small copper coins, which make a penny. And he called his disciples to him and said to them, 'Truly, I say to you, this poor widow has put in more than all those who are contributing to the offering box. For they all contributed out of their abundance, but she out of her poverty has put in everything she had, all she had to live on.'"
(Mark 12:41–44, ESV)

Many people think they're doing God a favor when they give Him whatever is left over after they pay their bills, but that doesn't take much faith to do. Instead, pray and ask God what you should give before you pay your bills. Doing that will ensure your offering isn't determined by what you don't have. Always let God lead you regarding what you should give and to whom you should give it.

Believe for the return when you give, because His Word promises it.

"Give, and it shall be given unto you; good measure, pressed down, and shaken together, and running over, shall men give into your bosom. For with the same measure that ye mete withal it shall be measured to you again."
(Luke 6:38, KJV 1900)

You shouldn't try to figure out how God will multiply the offering back to you. That's His business, not yours. Your job is to trust Him for the return on your giving.

Remember what we learned in the previous chapter on tithing. Malachi 3:10-12 tells us that when we bring the tithes and offerings into the storehouse, He will open the windows of heaven and pour out a blessing. He promises to rebuke the devourer for your sake.

> *"Bring ye all the tithes into the storehouse, That there may be meat in mine house, And prove me now herewith, saith the LORD of hosts, If I will not open you the windows of heaven, And pour you out a blessing, that there shall not be room enough to receive it. And I will rebuke the devourer for your sakes, And he shall not destroy the fruits of your ground; Neither shall your vine cast her fruit before the time in the field, saith the LORD of hosts. And all nations shall call you blessed: For ye shall be a delightsome land, saith the LORD of hosts."*
> (Malachi 3:10–12, KJV 1900)

There are many takeaways in this chapter, so I'll summarize them here.

- First, your offering must be worth something to you. It won't be worth anything to God, either, if it's not worth anything to you.
- You must make sure your heart is right before you give. You must make it right before giving your offering if your brother has anything against you.
- You must give your offering willingly.

- You must base your offering on what you have and not on what you don't have. Determine what you'll give before you sit down to pay your bills. That determination should be based on what God has told you to give and where to give it.

- Believe for the return on your offering.

God has an amazing financial plan for His children, but many never experience it because they haven't learned what His Word says about it. I hope this chapter will open your eyes to God's will and God's ways regarding giving because it opens an avenue of blessing unmatched by any investment returns you can acquire in the world.

Chapter Eight: Be Anxious For Nothing

ANXIETY HAS BECOME SO COMMON TODAY THAT MOST PEOple don't give it a second thought. It's as normal to them as eating and sleeping. However, anxiety is a deadly poison: It wreaks havoc physically, mentally, emotionally, and in every other way. It's a serious issue in the body of Christ, and it finds its root in unfounded fear, meaning that when you're operating in anxiety, you're usually afraid that something will happen that you don't want to happen, that something won't happen that you want to happen, or that whatever happens won't happen the way you want.

You can't medicate your way out of it. You can mask the symptoms with medication or even learn to cope, but doing so doesn't address the root cause. Anxiety can eventually kill you if left untreated. At a minimum, it causes high blood pressure, heart palpitations, and a host of other physical and emotional issues. It keeps Christians from moving forward in God's plan for their lives. Therefore, you must not accept it as a way of life. It isn't something you live with it like a wart or a birthmark. You don't manage or tolerate it, and it isn't part of your genetic material. Just because Mom and Grandma were worriers doesn't make it hereditary. It isn't.

There's a lack of trust in God at some underlying level when you function from a place of anxiety. You think that there's something that He cannot or will not take care of. You probably believe that He can and will redeem you, that you'll have eternal life, but you think that He just doesn't have what it takes to get you through the situation you're facing. That isn't true: God cares about every situation you face, regardless of how small it might be. He cares about the big stuff and the petty stuff.

What is God's perspective on fear? There are several hundred verses of Scripture in the Bible telling us not to worry. This should tell us that fear is a big deal to Him. And here's why. You're not in a place of faith, a place of trusting God when you're in a state of anxiety. You're not trusting Him to take care of the situation you're in. Nobody wants to admit that this is the root of the matter, but we must face this if we hope to have any relief from anxiety. God's will is that fear and anxiety not be part of the believer's life.

We can see that anxiety shouldn't be a condition of our lives when we look at John 14:27. That verse of Scripture says:

> *"Peace I leave with you, my peace I give unto you: not as the world giveth, give I unto you. Let not your heart be troubled, neither let it be afraid."*
> (John 14:27, KJV 1900)

Thus, peace should be the condition of our lives. The good news is that there's a scriptural prescription for anxiety because the Word of God is the best anxiety medication. How can I say that? Because Proverbs 4:20-22 says:

> *"My son, attend to my words; Incline thine ear unto my sayings. Let them not depart from thine eyes; Keep them in the midst of thine heart. For they are life unto those that find them, And health to all their flesh."*
> (Proverbs 4:20–22, KJV 1900)

Jesus died to purchase not just salvation for you but so many other things as well when He died on the cross. One of those things is peace of mind. Let's look at John 10:10 and 2 Timothy 1:7 to illustrate this point:

"The thief cometh not, but for to steal, and to kill, and to destroy: I am come that they might have life, and that they might have it more abundantly."
(John 10:10, KJV 1900)

"For God hath not given us the spirit of fear; but of power, and of love, and of a sound mind."
(2 Timothy 1:7, KJV 1900)

God's perspective is that His children should operate from a base of power, love, and self-discipline. The key to learning how to step into the abundance that Jesus died to bring you is to renew your mind with the Word of God. For the record, this isn't a suggestion. Let's look at what the Bible says in Romans 12:2, which says:

"And be not conformed to this world: but be ye transformed by the renewing of your mind, that ye may prove what is that good, and acceptable, and perfect, will of God."
(Romans 12:2, KJV 1900)

There's one thing I need to point out that will cut to the heart of this matter. We see it in Hebrews 11:6:

"Now without faith it is impossible to please him, for the one who approaches God must believe that he exists and is a rewarder of those who seek him."
(Hebrews 11:6, LEB)

Anxiety and fear are not faith, so we can conclude that neither of them pleases Him. I'll take this one step further. Romans 14:23 says that whatever isn't of faith is sin. I tell you this not to condemn you, but to help you to realize that you must not tolerate anxiety and fear.

The goal of this chapter is to show you what the Word says and how to apply it to your everyday life so you don't have to live as a victim of the enemy's strategies. Fear and anxiety are key weapons he uses to disrupt our lives, but you can fight back with scriptural weapons. You need not fall victim to fear and anxiety any longer.

God offers so many promises of peace and well-being in the Bible, but many people aren't experiencing them. Why? Because we have failed on our side. Many don't realize that anxiety truly is a sin in God's eyes because it's not faith. Too many pastors don't teach the truth of God's Word on this matter, so their congregations go from day to day experiencing anxiety and fear without realizing what it really is. Sure, we'll criticize those who lie, cheat, and steal, but we don't call anxiety what it really is. It's one of those little white sins that no one, supposedly, really cares about. Perhaps you don't know that the enemy kills the plan of God in believers' lives by getting them to give in to anxiety and fear.

Let's take a brief look at how detrimental fear can be by looking at Judges 13. I'll paraphrase here to save time, but I encourage you to read this chapter carefully and with an eye to the danger of fear. This chapter shows the Lord speaking to Moses and telling him to send twelve spies to spy out the land that God had said He was giving to them. He instructed them to look it over. He didn't say that He might give it to them; He said that He was giving it to them, and He told them that before they ever went. His perspective was that all they needed to do was claim what was theirs. Yet what happened? Ten of the twelve spies came back and called God a liar. They said that they weren't able to take it.

The problem didn't stop there. The ten spies giving the negative report not only poisoned their own minds, but they also poisoned the minds of the rest of the people children of Israel, causing them to rebel against the Lord. This ultimately caused them to wander in the wilderness for forty years until all those twenty years old and above had died off except for Joshua and Caleb. So, I ask you: Was fear a big deal to God in this case?

Similarly, the consequences can be just as severe as what we're reading about here for many people who hear the voice of God on a matter but fail to act. So many people forfeit the will of God for their lives because they're afraid to follow His directions. They wander in a wilderness for years, and some never come out of it. Thus, you can see why anxiety is not only harmful to our physical bodies, but it's also a killer of God's plans and purposes in our lives.

Let's look at a situation when someone stood against fear and saw God work in his favor. Genesis 26 tells us of a famine in the land during the days of Isaac. Isaac did what any reasonable person would do and went where there was hope, which was the land of Egypt. However, the Lord told him not to go to Egypt but to live where He had said to live, and He promised to bless him. Rather than surrender to fear and go to Egypt during the famine, Isaac sowed in the land as God instructed and reaped a hundredfold that same year. It pays to trust God, doesn't it?

I'd like to share a brief story from my life that illustrates that what happened to Isaac wasn't a fluke or a onetime miracle. I already used this example in an earlier chapter, but please bear with me, because that same example applies here. Many years ago, the place where I worked went through an acquisition. The acquirer offered me a job, but the Lord told me to decline it, take my severance package, and leave. What you need to know is that this was during the days of economic crisis. Jobs were scarce, so you could easily say that a famine was in force. Only a fool would decline a generous job offer without another job to replace it, but I knew what the Lord had said. When I asked Him what I was to do, His simple reply was, "Trust Me; I already have something for you."

I struggled with what He had told me and experienced severe anxiety. I looked at the job market and saw a job famine, but I decided I would go with God regardless of what happened to me. So be it if I failed and lost everything. I would experience what He said He had for me, or He would have to listen to me beg and plead for deliverance. What caused me to take the chance was the fact that I had read so many times about how the children of Israel wandered in the wilderness because of their unbelief in the Lord's promise. I didn't want to wander, so I gave my notice, took my severance package, and left.

I naively thought I would be back to work within a few weeks, but the weeks stretched into months. I studied the Word and prayed during that time. When I asked the Lord what was going on, all He would say is to trust Him, that He already had something for me. My faith started to waiver after eight months had passed, and I asked the Lord for help. I reminded Him I was running out of money from the severance package. He told me I would receive a phone call from someone I knew, that they would offer a job during that call, and that I was to accept it. He also said that I wouldn't run out of money. Sure enough, the call He had promised came a short time later. They offered me a job, I accepted, and I never ran out of money.

I told that story so I could say this: God is the only one who knows all things. You can't rely on what you know, what you see, or even the advice of others to get you through life. Jesus purchased something special for you when He died on the cross. Let's look at John 16:7, where Jesus is speaking.

"Nevertheless I tell you the truth; It is expedient for you that I go away: for if I go not away, the Comforter will not come unto you; but if I depart, I will send him unto you."
(John 16:7, KJV 1900)

Jesus makes a bold promise in John 16:13:

> *"Howbeit when he, the Spirit of truth, is come, he will guide you into all truth: for he shall not speak of himself; but whatsoever he shall hear, that shall he speak: and he will shew you things to come."*
> *(John 16:13, KJV 1900)*

The truth of these verses is repeatedly borne out in my life, and I know of many others who would say the same thing. It requires faith to act when God asks you to do something against the conventional wisdom. Wisdom dictated that Isaac should go to Egypt, but God said otherwise. In my life, only a complete fool would decline a job offer and not look for work when the country was in the midst of an epic economic crisis. Yet, Isaac fared well and so did I, and so will you if you'll trust God.

There's a Bible story in Genesis 12, verses 1-4, that I use to teach people that God can be trusted. It tells us of how God spoke to Abram and told him to leave his family behind and go to a place that He would show him. What many people miss about this passage is that Abram didn't know where he was going. Let's read it together:

> *"Now the LORD had said unto Abram, Get thee out of thy country, and from thy kindred, and from thy father's house, unto a land that I will shew thee: And I will make of thee a great nation, and I will bless thee, and make thy name great; and thou shalt be a blessing: And I will bless them that bless thee, and curse him that curseth thee: and in thee shall all families of the earth be blessed. So Abram departed, as the LORD had spoken unto him; and Lot went with him: and Abram was seventy and five years old when he departed out of Haran."*
> *(Genesis 12:1–4, KJV 1900)*

We know Abraham didn't know where he was going because it says in Hebrews 11:8 that:

"By faith Abraham, when he was called, obeyed to go out to a place that he was going to receive for an inheritance, and he went out, not knowing where he was going."
(Hebrews 11:8, LEB)

It took a lot of faith for Abraham to follow God without knowing where he was going, but he did it, and he's considered the father of faith. My point for bringing this up is that God will often only show you the first step you are to take. He won't show you the next step until you take the first one. That's where many people fail: They refuse to take the first step because they don't know what the next step will be. They want to know every step in the plan before they'll make a move, but that's not usually how God does it. He requires us to step out in faith when He gives us direction. Remember, faith pleases Him.

Let me assure you that doubts will probably plague you as you do what the Lord tells you to do, especially when it seems strange. However, feeling fear differs from giving in to it. Many times in the Bible, people were told to "fear not," which means that they felt fear. This command was a directive to not give in to it, which means don't get into guilt and condemnation whenever you feel fear. The key is not to let it get a hold of you and prevent you from doing what the Lord tells you. Stand against fear. A teacher I admire deeply has said that when the Lord asked her to do something out of the ordinary, she told herself to "Do it afraid." I use that phrase today because it's so appropriate.

Now I'd like to take you through a few scriptural examples of situations when anxiety and worry were present and what the solution is. Let's start in Luke, Chapter 10, verses 38 to 42.

"Now as they traveled along, he entered into a certain village. And a certain woman named Martha welcomed him. And she had a sister named Mary, who also sat at the feet of Jesus and was listening to his teaching. But Martha was distracted with much preparation, so she approached and said, "Lord, is it not a concern to you that my sister has left me alone to make preparations? Then tell her that she should help me!" But the Lord answered and said to her, "Martha, Martha, you are anxious and troubled about many things! But few things are necessary, or only one thing, for Mary has chosen the better part, which will not be taken away from her.""

(Luke 10:38–42, LEB)

Martha was in a state of anxiety. This might seem like a minor example, but we must keep in mind that anxiety can be present in major and minor situations. It's really a matter of degree here.

We see that Martha confronted the Lord and asked Him to command Mary to help with the serving when we unpack these verses. Yet, He chastised her instead. He told her that Mary had chosen the good thing, and He wasn't about to take that away from her. The interesting thing to note here is that Martha was attempting to serve the Lord, so it isn't like she wasn't doing something meaningful. We can conclude from what the Lord said that He wasn't concerned about her serving Him from a hospitality perspective. That wasn't His priority, nor should it have been her priority. We must keep in mind that we can do good things, but they might not be things He considers important.

He was speaking about the Kingdom of God when He said that Mary chose the good thing. Martha was trying to serve the Lord with good hospitality, but what He wanted was for her to sit down with Him, as her sister Mary had chosen to do. Matthew 6:33 provides insight into what that means. It says:

"But seek first the Kingdom of God and his righteousness, and all these things will be added to you."
(Matthew 6:33, ESV)

When we seek first the Kingdom of God and His righteousness, all the other things— what we eat, drink, and wear— are added as a pleasant side effect of that. Those verses in Matthew 6:25-31 that say not to worry about your life, what you'll eat or drink, or what you'll wear are <u>not</u> suggestions: They're commands. It's a sin to function in opposition to that command. That's a fact whether we like it or not.

Let's read the verses through together, understanding that they're a Biblical command.

"Therefore I say unto you, Take no thought for your life, what ye shall eat, or what ye shall drink; nor yet for your body, what ye shall put on. Is not the life more than meat, and the body than raiment? Behold the fowls of the air: for they sow not, neither do they reap, nor gather into barns; yet your heavenly Father feedeth them. Are ye not much better than they? Which of you by taking thought can add one cubit unto his stature? And why take ye thought for raiment? Consider the lilies of the field, how they grow; they toil not, neither do they spin: And yet I say unto you, That even Solomon in all his glory was not arrayed like one of these. Wherefore, if God so clothe the grass of the field, which to day is, and to morrow is cast into the oven, shall he not much more clothe you, O ye of little faith? Therefore take no thought, saying, What shall we eat? or, What shall we drink? or, Wherewithal shall we be clothed? (For after all these things do the Gentiles seek:) for your heavenly Father knoweth that ye have need of all these things. But seek ye first the Kingdom of God, and his righteousness;

and all these things shall be added unto you."
(Matthew 6:25–33, KJV 1900)

A logical question now might be, "How do I put this into practical application?", so let's use two different Scriptures:

"Casting down imaginations, and every high thing that exalteth itself against the knowledge of God, and bringing into captivity every thought to the obedience of Christ;"
(2 Corinthians 10:5, KJV 1900)

Let's first discuss a couple of key definitions. "Casting down" is best explained by using an example. Let's say you're sitting in a chair and you get the creepy sensation of an insect crawling in your hair. You reach up, feel around until you take hold of it, and then throw it to the ground to get it away from you as quickly as possible. In this example, you have 'cast down' the insect that was crawling in your hair. Therefore, 'casting down' carries with it the idea of taking hold of something and throwing it to the ground. "Imaginations" is defined in several dictionaries in a variety of ways, but boils down to mental images or concepts of what isn't present to the senses, meaning that it doesn't currently exist. It would say something like this in modern language:

"Take hold of those thoughts or imaginations that don't line up with the Word of God and throw them to the ground."

The next logical question would be, "How do I do that?". You do it by replacing the negative thought with what the Word says. How would the Word of God do this, you might ask? Because Hebrews 4:12 says:

"For the word of God is living and active and sharper than any double-edged sword, and piercing as far as the division of soul and spirit, both joints and marrow, and able to judge the reflections and thoughts of the heart."
(Hebrews 4:12, LEB)

We need to look at Philippians 4:6-8 to understand how to deal with anxiety. We'll focus on these verses because they contain the critical keys to addressing anxiety.

"Be anxious for nothing, but in everything by prayer and supplication with thanksgiving let your requests be made known to God. And the peace of God that surpasses all understanding will guard your hearts and your minds in Christ Jesus. Finally, brothers, whatever things are true, whatever things are honorable, whatever things are right, whatever things are pure, whatever things are pleasing, whatever things are commendable, if there is any excellence of character and if anything praiseworthy, think about these things."
(Philippians 4:6–8, LEB)

Let's break down the steps together:

1. Be anxious for nothing. In modern language, we would say "Don't be anxious about anything— don't worry." You must bring the situation before God in prayer and petition (supplication) to be able to do that. "Petition" refers to a particular need, so don't be vague; be as specific as you know how to be.

2. The next part is to offer that prayer with thanksgiving. Thank Him for hearing you and for caring about you. Expect the peace of God to guard your heart and mind. Declare out loud that His peace guards your heart and mind.

3. Make sure that you think on things that are true, honest, just, pure, lovely, and of good report. Whatever you think about needs to meet all of those conditions.
   Verse 8 focuses on what you're thinking about. Remember

> that it says "think on these things". This tells us that our thought life is critical, but it's influenced by all of your senses. The examples I'll use below deal with what we see and what we hear.

Just because you hear something that's true doesn't mean you should listen to it. The world news is an example. The way news is reported is bound to bring anxiety, with all the talk of wars, epidemics, and shootings, so be careful how much news you consume each day. Frankly, I recommend eliminating the news altogether for a while so you can test the impact it has on you if you frequently struggle with anxiety. I'm not suggesting that you be ignorant of what's going on in the world, but I am saying to find news outlets that bring balanced reporting to you. Focus on God's Word and not the world's word.

The music you listen to might also be a problem, and I'm not just referring to death metal or heavy metal. It can be any music that influences your mood negatively. The next time you startup your song playlist, pay careful attention to how the songs make you feel. Sad songs will make you feel sad. Angry, hateful songs will make you feel angry and hateful. And so on. The lyrics are written that way for a reason, so be very careful what you listen to. The Scriptural admonition in Mark 4:24 to "take heed what you hear" applies here. I usually recommend that anyone suffering from anxiety or panic attacks change from their current playlist of hard rock, classic rock, pop music, or whatever genre they're listening to, to something more uplifting, such as gospel or worship music. This one minor change had a positive impact on each person who acted on my recommendation without exception. However, some Christians don't particularly care for gospel or worship music outside of church, so I would recommend trying soft, classical music. I also encourage people to listen to the Bible on CD or audio sessions of their favorite Christian teachings. These are great ways to keep your mind renewed with the Word, especially for moments when you're feeling anxious.

One reason I emphasize the importance of what you listen to is because Romans 10:17 says:

"So then faith cometh by hearing,
and hearing by the word of God."
(Romans 10:17, KJV 1900)

Faith comes by what you hear, and that can be for good or bad. You can have positive faith, or you can have negative faith. Let me explain. You'll develop the right faith if you listen to things that are uplifting, such as the Word of God. Negative faith, or fear, results if you listen to negative things, and it manifests as anxiety, fear, or depression. Thus, it is critically important to be careful of everything you hear.

TV is another medium you need to be careful of. What shows do you watch? Do they meet the conditions of Philippians 4:8? Are they true, honest, just, pure, lovely, and of a good report? Consider eliminating them from your life if they're not. You'll need to make some tough decisions about what you watch if you're serious about eradicating fear and anxiety from your life. Horror movies and movies with lots of violence, killing, and blood won't help you keep peace in your life. The real question is, "How badly do you want freedom from anxiety?"

I'd like to offer some ideas about how to handle this at home and when you're out. Excuse yourself and go into another room to study the Word or do something else until the movie is over if you live in a household where you're not the ultimate authority over what you watch. Not all of us have Bible-believing people in our lives, so I don't recommend that you start an argument over it or try to enforce your position on the matter. This has happened to me several times over the years, and I have found that when I do this often enough, the people who wanted to watch those movies will wait until I'm not around to watch them. They'll usually say instead that they'll watch that movie some other time.

I do this at relatives' houses, too. I'll grab a book and go read it out of earshot of the movie if they insist on watching something that I don't want to watch. I refuse to start arguments over something like this, but I won't compromise my beliefs, either. The decision to watch is ultimately mine. We need to remember that not all of us have saved family members, so we must draw a line between giving in to their worldly habits and staying congruent with our own convictions. I know of some people who would start an argument over it, but it rarely serves a godly purpose. I choose an approach that pulls me away from the environment in which I don't wish to be, yet doesn't start an argument with family members.

Always let it go when you're trying to decide whether to start a fight or keep the peace, because having a graceful, merciful attitude when in the presence of sinners will do more to win them than having an angry, Pharisaical attitude. Speaking from experience, when I gracefully explain that I'd prefer not to watch a certain type of movie, my family members will either change the channel to something that I can watch, or they'll proceed to watch it and I'll go somewhere else until it's over. This usually happens if there are several people who want to watch it. I refuse to become angry and offended when that happens, but again, the choice to watch is yours, so choose wisely.

This next recommendation is tough. If you spend time with people who do nothing but bring you down and suck the life out of you, consider whether that relationship needs to remain a part of your life. This isn't a simple thing to do, and I understand that, but if you truly want to live free from anxiety, this is also something to consider. 1 Corinthians 15:33 issues a stern warning about the company we keep:

"Do not be deceived! "Bad company corrupts good morals.""
(1 Corinthians 15:33, LEB)

In other words, you must be very careful about who you spend time with.

Another thing that can bring unnecessary anxiety is focusing on too many things at once. The world calls it multitasking, but it can cause you to feel fragmented. Try to keep your focus on one thing at a time. I encourage people to organize their day as much as possible and allow buffer time so that they can accomplish what needs to be done. However, so many people try to schedule every minute of their day with no margin at all. You've automatically set yourself up for failure when you do that. There's no way to have a life when every minute is scheduled. Leave room for the unexpected. Learning to schedule your day properly isn't a waste of time; it's effective time management. You wonder how you'll get it all done when your day is over scheduled, and you finally end up in a state of anxiety over it.

Being reactionary is another thing that can cause problems. Some people react rather than respond to the issues of life. Many people think they're the same thing, but they're not. The best way that I can explain it is that reactionary people don't think before acting. They don't stop to assess the meaning of the event and consider the options for handling it when faced with a situation that would naturally bring on fear or anxiety. Instead, they freak out.

Responsive people take a moment to assess what they've heard. They ask, "What does the Bible say about that? How would the Lord want me to handle this?" They ask the Holy Spirit for guidance, they don't say the first thing that comes to mind, especially if it won't glorify God.

Let me give you an example. Let's say that you encounter a problem on the job that you don't know how to handle. Your choice is to let fear and anxiety overtake you, which is a reactive response, or you can stop, go to a private place and pray in the Holy Spirit for guidance on what to do. I recommend saying something like this in situations where you're being pressed for a response: "I don't have an answer right at the moment, but I'll get back to you in a few minutes." Once I say that, I'll excuse myself and go pray about the situation. It's never failed, but if I say whatever comes to mind, especially if I'm angry, I'll usually make it worse.

Proverbs 29:11 says that a fool vents his feelings. Some people say whatever is on their mind and call it venting, but you can see what the Bible has to say about that. Always take a moment to consider a response rather than just reacting. Being responsive instead of reactionary is a skill that can be learned; it's just a matter of practice. Saying that you can't help it discounts what the Bible says you should do, so go with the Biblical example.

Inspect these areas to see if any of them fit your situation. I need to emphasize that this isn't an exhaustive list of things to watch out for, but they're the common things that people face. View this list as a starting point and go from there.

There's one more area I want to touch on before we go over the final list of steps for combatting anxiety: It pertains to forgiveness. More often than not, people have several areas of their emotional life that need correcting before they're in any position to address anxiety. Forgiveness is one topic that always comes up. You might wonder why it makes a difference with anxiety, so let's look at the Scriptural basis for why it has everything to do with it. Let's look at Mark 11:24-25.

> *"Therefore I say to you, whatever things you ask when you pray, believe that you receive them, and you'll have them. "And whenever you stand praying, if you have anything against anyone, forgive him, that your Father in heaven may also forgive you your trespasses."*
> *(Mark 11:24–25, NKJV)*

We often hear throughout the Christian world about Mark 11:24 as the "name it and claim it" Scripture, but I'd like you to look past that so that we can glean valuable insight about prayer. Let's zero in on verse 25, which says that when you stand praying, you must forgive, so that God might forgive your sins. Note that God won't forgive your sins if you won't forgive others. That verse is also a continuation of verse 24, so it means that in order for God to hear your prayers, you must forgive, and you must forgive others of all their sins, not just the small stuff.

How does this relate to our discussion about anxiety? Philippians 4:6-7 tells us to come to God in prayer. Yet, now we see from the verses in Mark that when we stand praying, we must forgive. So, the two do indeed go hand in hand.

From everything we've discussed so far, we've learned that we must:

- Not be anxious about anything. That's a command, not a suggestion.

- Bring the situation before God in prayer, being as specific as you know how to be.

- Offer that prayer with thanksgiving, thanking Him for hearing you and caring about you.

- Expect the peace of God to guard your heart and mind. This verse says that will happen if you do your part, so expect the peace of God to guard you.

- Make sure that you think on things that are true, honest, just, pure, lovely, and of good report. Your prayer must meet all of those conditions.

- Forgive if you have anything against anyone. This is not a suggestion, but a requirement.

You'll develop the right faith for how to deal with anxiety if you'll commit to taking the steps provided in this chapter, which gives you the Word of God about anxiety. Anxiety isn't easily overcome, especially if it's been a part of your life for any length of time. However, the Word of God has the answer to combating anxiety, so use it to your advantage, because you shouldn't accept it as a condition of your life.

Be willing to wait on the Lord for an answer after you've prayed, as just outlined. Ask the Holy Spirit for guidance about how to handle the issues you face. Let Him lead you instead of letting the enemy lead you. There is no situation that you and the Lord cannot face together. Nothing happens that takes the Lord by surprise, so let Him help you. He gave the Comforter, the Holy Spirit, as a Companion, so let Him be that for you.

Keep a journal of what the Holy Spirit speaks to you as you put these concepts into practice and keep a record of the times when the Lord has come through for you. Your memory of them fades if you don't document the accounts of His faithfulness. Write them down. Read your journal often, because it helps to remind you that He's not far off; He's with you, and He cares about you. Keeping a record of His goodness does much to combat anxiety because it serves as a reminder of His goodness.

Here's a prayer you can use when anxiety tries to come over you. You can use it as often as you'd like.

"Heavenly Father, I thank You for Your Word, that it has an answer for every issue of life, and that includes anxiety. I know Jesus died so that I could live free from fear. You haven't given me the spirit of fear, so I refuse to allow anxiety to continue in my life. Instead, I will operate from a spirit of power, love, and a sound mind, as it says in 2 Timothy 1:7. And to do that, I choose to renew my mind with what Your Word says about fear. I will not tolerate or manage it. It will have no place in my life. It's a tactic of the enemy to steal peace and joy from me, and I will not stand for it any longer.

I will not worry or have anxiety about anything. Instead, I will do as Your Word says. I will bring the situation to you in prayer with a humble heart and with thanksgiving, and Your peace, which passes all understanding, will keep my heart and mind through Christ Jesus.

I will focus my thoughts on things that are true, honest, just, pure, lovely, and of good report. And if there are areas of my life where you need me to make changes so that anxiety cannot creep in, then please reveal them to me. I don't want to live with anxiety any longer. Instead, I commit to live free from worry in the Name of Jesus. I walk in Your peace, which passes all understanding, and I declare I am free from worry, anxiety, and fear.

Finally, Father, I agree to be obedient to your Word regarding forgiveness. Your Word says that when I stand praying, I must forgive. Please help me search my heart for any areas of unforgiveness and help me forgive everyone who has wronged me. With Your help, I can and will remove this from my life.

Lord, I want to be free of the issues that weigh me down. If you'll guide me and show me what to do in this situation, then I commit to be obedient to the direction You provide.

I thank You, Father. In Jesus' Name I pray, amen."

Chapter Nine: Success God's Way

ACHIEVING SUCCESS GOD'S WAY RUNS COUNTER TO EVERYthing the world says to do. The world teaches to tout your achievements, to run over other people in your quest for the top rung of the ladder, and to compromise if you want to get ahead. God's way is the exact opposite of all that: Achieving success His way requires sacrifice, but the results far outweigh it. The concepts taught in this chapter may not make sense at first, but study them for yourself. Change your mindset to fit God's view of success, and then you can position yourself to receive all He has for you.

First, we'll talk about what not to do, because the Bible is clear. I'll provide examples of people who rebelled against God's purposes and who paid a high price. Then we'll talk about people who achieved success the right way. None became successful the easy way, not even Jesus. Each was tried and tested and ultimately promoted to a prominent position. These are the examples we should follow, not the abusive, corrupt methods used by so many today.

This chapter will also serve as a reminder to put God first and to seek His kingdom first, because that's all that matters. You'll want to hear the words, "Thou good and faithful servant" (Matthew 25:21) when the end of your life arrives. You won't want to hear the words that so many will hear because they failed to honor God. The Righteous Judge will say,

> *"Depart from Me, worker of iniquity, for I never knew you" (Matthew 7:23).*

Let's go back to the beginning, to the book of Genesis, to understand what not to do. Chapter 3 finds the serpent contradicting what God had told Adam and Eve. The serpent said they would not surely die but would be like God, knowing good and evil (Genesis 3:1-4). Eve ate, then gave some to her husband, and he also ate. Their eyes were opened, and the curse was loosed into the world. They became subject to death, and their lives would never be the same. From that point forward, the curse was on the earth, only to be overturned when Jesus came as the Lamb, slain before the foundation of the world.

What we all need to learn from this account is that obedience to God's commands isn't optional. There's a price to pay for disobedience. We might not always see the fruits of our actions immediately, but they will surely come. The repercussions can last for a long, long time even if we repent of our sins.

You can repent before God and receive forgiveness, but that doesn't mean that you get away with no consequences. Look no further than the account of David's sin with Bathsheba. Many people focus on the adulterous part of this story but forget that David had Bathsheba's husband, Uriah, sent to the front lines of battle so David could be sure that he died. That's cold-blooded murder, even if David didn't actually wield the instrument that caused Uriah's death. The fact is, he gave the order to put Uriah on the front lines, so he is ultimately responsible for the death of a faithful soldier.

Another tragic consequence of David's union with Bathsheba is the death of their first child, the one conceived because of adultery. Nathan the prophet advises David in 2 Samuel 12:14 that the child would die because his sin gave his enemies the opportunity to blaspheme God.

"Howbeit, because by this deed thou hast given great occasion to the enemies of the LORD to blaspheme, the child also that is born unto thee shall surely die."
(2 Samuel 12:14, KJV 1900)

David fasted and prayed for the life of his child, yet the child died.

Our next example is a cautionary tale of why partial obedience is still disobedience. Many times we think it's okay to obey God halfway, but it's not. We find the prophet Samuel advising King Saul in 1 Samuel 15 that God wanted the Amalekites destroyed because of their opposition to the Israelites when they came out of Egypt. Samuel told Saul that all the inhabitants and the livestock were to be destroyed, so Saul mobilized his armies and went against them.

However, Saul made a grave mistake: He spared King Ahab and kept the best of the sheep and oxen, even though he was fully aware of God's command to utterly destroy the people and the livestock. The Lord then tells Samuel that He had rejected Saul from being king any longer. The prophet delivers the message to Saul, along with the chilling declaration that his rebellion is just as sinful as witchcraft and his stubbornness as worshiping idols. Saul admits his sin, but it's too late. There's no going back.

Sometimes we think that partial obedience to a command of God is no big deal, but it cost Saul his kingdom. Let the story of King Saul serve as a reminder of the consequences if you're tempted to partially obey God. Remember: you probably won't know the repercussions until the damage is done.

Obedience to God must come before anything else. The world's ways will creep in and taint the plan of God for your life if your heart isn't right before Him. His plans and His ways must be what you seek after, not your own selfish ambitions.

The subordination of one's will makes the average Christian nervous. Why? Because then you'd have to wonder: Is it possible that God might ask you to do something you don't want to do? The answer is yes.

I've heard it said that God will never ask you to do something you don't want to do. I've even heard it in times past from well-meaning preachers. Every time I hear or read about someone making that statement, it concerns me because it's not true.

The fact is, God does ask us to do things we don't want to do from time to time. I give you the prophet Jonah as an example. He fled in the opposite direction when God asked him to deliver a message to the inhabitants of Nineveh.

"Now the word of the LORD came unto Jonah the son of Amittai, saying, Arise, go to Nineveh, that great city, and cry against it; for their wickedness is come up before me. But Jonah rose up to flee unto Tarshish from the presence of the LORD, and went down to Joppa; and he found a ship going to Tarshish: so he paid the fare thereof, and went down into it, to go with them unto Tarshish from the presence of the LORD."
(Jonah 1:1–3, KJV 1900)

Jonah ended up in the belly of a whale over his disobedience, though he did eventually comply with God's wishes.

I'm not sure how we can read verses like these and get the impression that God won't ask us to do things we don't want to do. Clearly, He does. God has purposes that need to be accomplished on the Earth, and He uses people to accomplish them. Sometimes those purposes include asking us to do things we don't want to do.

The best example of all is our Lord and Savior, Jesus Christ. He sweat drops of blood in the garden of Gethsemane over the prospect of what He was about to do. Does this suggest that He wanted to do it? It doesn't.

However, He was willing. He laid down His own will to do the will of the Father.

"And he was withdrawn from them about a stone's cast, and kneeled down, and prayed, Saying, Father, if thou be willing, remove this cup from me: nevertheless not my will, but thine, be done."
(Luke 22:41–42, KJV 1900)

If we wanted to do everything God asked us to do, we probably wouldn't have verses like Isaiah 1:19 telling us we'll eat the good of the land if we're willing and obedient. For the record, there's a world of difference between being willing to do something and wanting to do it. So, don't let anyone fool you into thinking that God won't ask you to do something you don't want to do. He can.

God's plans and purposes are not for the faint of heart. Many average Christians go through life having never accomplished what God wanted them to do. However, those who are part of the faith hall of fame underwent tests and trials and came out on the other side, having run the race given to them by God. They went where the Lord told them to go, and they did what He told them to do. The call of God on your life might be the exact opposite of what you wanted for your life, but you'll be much better off going where He tells you to go, because there's no prize for running the race you designed for yourself.

Pride is one thing that can derail God's plan for your life. It's one thing that's common in the workplace today, and it's mainly because many operate under the assumption that they must make everyone aware of their accomplishments in order to receive a promotion. The problem with this is that it usually manifests in bragging, which runs counter to what the Bible says.

"Lift not up your horn on high: Speak not with a stiff neck. For promotion cometh neither from the east, Nor from the west, nor from the south. But God is the judge: He putteth down one, and setteth up another."
(Psalm 75:5–7, KJV 1900)

You don't need to promote yourself. God can find you if He can find David on the backside of a mountain tending sheep. Your obligation is to follow the leading of the Lord and to humble yourself before Him.

"Humble yourselves before the Lord, and he will exalt you."
(James 4:10, ESV)

"One's pride will bring him low, but he who is lowly in spirit will obtain honor."
(Proverbs 29:23, ESV)

Pride won't gain a foothold in your life if you'll continually humble yourself. You'll be in the right place at the right time if you'll completely subordinate your will to His.

Now we'll turn our attention to the things you should be doing in order to run the race God designed for you. One of those things is to always put God first. This means that you should go after God, not after promotion. You should only want the promotion that God gives. God will add everything you need, which includes promotion, if you'll seek first His kingdom and His way of doing things. The subject of putting God first is addressed in another chapter, but it won't hurt to review it briefly again.

"But seek first his kingdom and righteousness, and all these things will be added to you."
(Matthew 6:33, LEB)

Remember that seeking God first isn't a suggestion. It's a command, so we shouldn't look at it as optional. You'll be on track to have things added to you, in God's perfect timing and in His perfect way, if you'll set your heart and mind to doing this with all your heart.

Obedience isn't always easy. God commanded Abram to move away from his relatives and away from the country where he was living to a place God would show him.

"Now the LORD said to Abram, "Go from
your country and your kindred and your father's house ***to***
the land that I will show you.*"*
(Genesis 12:1, ESV, emphasis added)

This means that Abram had to leave without knowing the destination in advance. He had to trust that God would show him the way. History bears out that God showed him the way, and Abram received God's promises. This is when being willing and obedient will cause you to eat the good of the land (Isaiah 1:19). Abram, whose name was later changed to Abraham, did indeed eat the good of the land, because he became very wealthy. Best of all, he became the father of many nations, as God promised beforehand.

Another aspect of success God's way requires us to have the heart of a servant. Many so-called leaders treat those under them as though they were nothing more than tools. I've seen this so many times, even with those who consider themselves Christian leaders. This wasn't how Jesus led, and if He didn't lead that way, then neither should we.

"It shall not be so among you. But whoever
would be great among you must be your servant, and
whoever would be first among you must be your
slave, even as the Son of Man came not to be
served but to serve, and to

give his life as a ransom for many.'"
(Matthew 20:26–28, ESV)

"For who is the greater, one who reclines at table or one who serves? Is it not the one who reclines at table? But I am among you as the one who serves."
(Luke 22:27, ESV)

"Have this mind among yourselves, which is yours in Christ Jesus, who, though he was in the form of God, didn't count equality with God a thing to be grasped, but emptied himself, by taking the form of a servant, being born in the likeness of men. And being found in human form, he humbled himself by becoming obedient to the point of death, even death on a cross. Therefore God has highly exalted him and bestowed on him the name that is above every name,"
(Philippians 2:5–9, ESV)

Leadership over others isn't about power; it's about sacrificing yourself for the good of those you lead. It means putting their needs ahead of yours. There are so many things that could be said about leadership, but this chapter isn't meant to be a treatise on the subject, so I'll simply mention this: If you're called to a position of leadership, remember that it's about serving, not about ruling harshly over others. Jesus was the supreme example of leadership, so take the time to study how He did it and copy His methods.

We're going to look at a few examples of people who did it the right way. They stayed with the plan of God through good times and bad and ultimately won the prize.

Many of us are familiar with the story of Joseph. He was Jacob's (Israel's) favorite, which caused his brothers to hate him.

"Now Israel loved Joseph more than all his children, because he was the son of his old age: and he made him a coat of many colours. And when his brethren saw that their father loved him more than all his brethren, they hated him, and could not speak peaceably unto him."
(Genesis 37:3–4, KJV 1900)

God gave Joseph a dream of his future, which he shared with his brothers. They were already jealous of him, but now he had the audacity to tell them that they would bow down to him some day.

"And Joseph dreamed a dream, and he told it his brethren: and they hated him yet the more. And he said unto them, Hear, I pray you, this dream which I have dreamed: For, behold, we were binding sheaves in the field, and, lo, my sheaf arose, and also stood upright; and, behold, your sheaves stood round about, and made obeisance to my sheaf. And his brethren said to him, Shalt thou indeed reign over us? or shalt thou indeed have dominion over us? And they hated him yet the more for his dreams, and for his words."
(Genesis 37:5–8, KJV 1900)

One day, his father asked him to check on his brothers who were out feeding the flock. They made plans to get rid of him when they saw him approaching. They threw him into a pit, then sold him to some Midianites. He was taken to Egypt and sold to Potiphar, a captain of the guards. Potiphar saw God was with Joseph, so he put him in charge over all his household. However, Potiphar's wife wanted Joseph because he was handsome. She accused him of rape when he refused to give in to her demands, and he was thrown into prison for a crime he didn't commit. God showed him favor with the keeper of the prison while he was there.

Fast forward several years. The King of Egypt's cupbearer and baker were thrown into prison for offending their master. Each had a dream while there. Joseph interpreted the cupbearer's dream by telling him he would be restored to his former position in three days. He told the baker that he would be hanged within the same timeframe. Joseph begged the cupbearer not to forget him, but that's exactly what he did.

Two more years elapsed, and Pharaoh had a disturbing dream that nobody could interpret. It was then that the cupbearer remembered what Joseph did for him. He told his master that Joseph could tell him what his dream meant. Joseph was brought from prison, cleaned up, and presented to Pharaoh. When the dream was told to him, Joseph interpreted it to mean that seven years of plenty would be followed by seven years of famine. He advised Pharaoh to set someone over the land of Egypt to store up a percentage of the food during the good years so it would be available to sustain the people during the famine.

Pharaoh saw Joseph's wisdom and put him in charge. He went from the prison to the palace within one day, though his journey along the way had been a hard one. God's plans and purposes for your life may mean that you won't walk on a bed of roses, but if you'll do it His way, favor will follow you, just as it did with Joseph. Always follow the methods outlined in the Bible: You'll never go wrong, and you'll achieve success God's way if you do.

CHAPTER TEN: The Art Of Forgiveness

WE'LL EXPLORE THE CONCEPT OF FORGIVENESS IN THIS CHAPter and what it means from a scriptural perspective, because there's a misunderstanding in the Body of Christ about this critical topic. Therefore, let's settle something at the outset: If you choose God, you must also choose His ways. Joshua challenged the people with this statement in Joshua 25:15:

"And if it seem evil unto you to serve the LORD, choose you this day whom ye will serve; whether the gods which your fathers served that were on the other side of the flood, or the gods of the Amorites, in whose land ye dwell: but as for me and my house, we will serve the LORD."
(Joshua 24:15, KJV 1900)

I offer you the same challenge. Will you serve God wholeheartedly? Let's dig deep into this matter of forgiveness if your answer is yes, because it's a subject that can be tough to take unless you decide in the beginning that you'll do whatever the Word says, regardless of how much your flesh rebels against it.

We'll start with a few critical verses to set the stage for our discussion.

"Therefore I say unto you, What things soever ye desire, when ye pray, believe that ye receive them, and ye shall have them. ***And when ye stand praying, forgive****, if ye have ought against any: that your Father also which is in heaven may forgive you your trespasses." (Mark 11:24–25, KJV 1900, emphasis added)*

Notice that this verse isn't saying to forgive if you feel like it. It's saying that you must forgive if you expect God to forgive your sins.

Before you become terribly upset at the requirement to forgive, I should mention that just because you forgive somebody who has wronged you doesn't mean that person gets away with anything. As an example, let's assume that someone robs your house and is apprehended by the police. That person may repent of their sin and be forgiven by God, but that doesn't mean they won't go to jail. God's forgiveness doesn't guarantee deliverance from the consequences of their actions. In no way does it absolve you of the requirement to forgive.

The offender must still answer to God even if the offense doesn't lead to justice in the earthly realm. He is the ultimate Judge of All.

"Dearly beloved, avenge not yourselves, but rather give place unto wrath: for it is written, Vengeance is mine; I will repay, saith the Lord."
(Romans 12:19, KJV 1900)

This verse of Scripture doesn't say that God will show you how He plans to repay. He says that vengeance is His and He will repay. We must take Him at His Word by faith and forgive as He directs us.

For the record, forgiveness is a decision and not a feeling. You can decide to forgive someone even though you don't feel like it. It can take time for your feelings to catch up with your words, but they will eventually come in line.

Let's look at some scriptural examples of forgiveness in action. These are extreme cases, and most of us will never experience this level of betrayal, but the Bible teaches in these instances that forgiveness is possible.

Jesus forgave even during the darkest hour of His life, when He submitted Himself to be tortured and killed on our behalf. Luke 23:34 recounts his Words:

> *"And Jesus said, "Father, forgive them, for they know not what they do." And they cast lots to divide his garments."*
> *(Luke 23:34, ESV)*

The Bible records that as the people stoned Stephen, he forgave.

> *"And as they were stoning Stephen, he called out, "Lord Jesus, receive my spirit." And falling to his knees he cried out with a loud voice, "Lord, do not hold this sin against them." And when he had said this, he fell asleep."*
> *(Acts 7:59–60, ESV)*

Another familiar Biblical account of forgiveness is found in the Book of Genesis, Chapter 37. Here we find the account of Joseph. He was sold into slavery by his brothers, then put into prison for a crime he didn't commit, yet he could still forgive those who did it.

> *"Now when they saw him afar off, even before he came near them, they conspired against him to kill him. Then they said to one another, "Look, this dreamer is coming! Come therefore, let us now kill him and cast him into some pit; and we shall say, 'Some wild beast has devoured him.' We shall see what will become of his dreams!" But Reuben heard it, and he delivered him out of their hands, and said,*

"Let us not kill him." And Reuben said to them, "Shed no blood, but cast him into this pit which is in the wilderness, and do not lay a hand on him"—that he might deliver him out of their hands, and bring him back to his father. So it came to pass, when Joseph had come to his brothers, that they stripped Joseph of his tunic, the tunic of many colors that was on him. Then they took him and cast him into a pit. And the pit was empty; there was no water in it. And they sat down to eat a meal. Then they lifted their eyes and looked, and there was a company of Ishmaelites, coming from Gilead with their camels, bearing spices, balm, and myrrh, on their way to carry them down to Egypt. So Judah said to his brothers, "What profit is there if we kill our brother and conceal his blood? Come and let us sell him to the Ishmaelites, and let not our hand be upon him, for he is our brother and our flesh." And his brothers listened. Then Midianite traders passed by; so the brothers pulled Joseph up and lifted him out of the pit, and sold him to the Ishmaelites for twenty shekels of silver. And they took Joseph to Egypt."

(Genesis 37:18–28, NKJV)

They committed still more wrongs against Joseph after this, but to save time, I won't go into them here. In the next set of verses, Joseph is second in command in Egypt and is a man with tremendous power and influence. Joseph's father died and his brothers were in a vulnerable position. He could take revenge if he wanted to, and there was nobody except the pharaoh himself who could stop him. Let's see what happens.

"When Joseph's brothers saw that their father was dead, they said, "Perhaps Joseph will hate us, and may actually repay us for all the evil which we did to him." So they sent messengers to Joseph, saying, "Before your father died

he commanded, saying, 'Thus you shall say to Joseph: "I beg you, please forgive the trespass of your brothers and their sin; for they did evil to you." ' Now, please, forgive the trespass of the servants of the God of your father." And Joseph wept when they spoke to him. Then his brothers also went and fell down before his face, and they said, "Behold, we are your servants." Joseph said to them, "Do not be afraid, ***for am I in the place of God? But as for you, you meant evil against me; but God meant it for good, in order to bring it about as it is this day, to save many people alive.*** *Now therefore, do not be afraid; I will provide for you and your little ones." And he comforted them and spoke kindly to them. So Joseph dwelt in Egypt, he and his father's household. And Joseph lived one hundred and ten years. Joseph saw Ephraim's children to the third generation. The children of Machir, the son of Manasseh, were also brought up on Joseph's knees."*
(Genesis 50:15–23, NKJV, emphasis added)

Joseph could have taken revenge against his brothers with the power he had, but he didn't. He understood he wasn't in the place of God. Thus, regardless of the wrongs done to us by others, we must remember these examples of forgiveness. Many of us will never have such horrible things done to us, but if Joseph can forgive, then so can we.

We also need to realize that forgiveness and reconciliation are not the same thing. You must forgive others for their trespasses against you, but you're not obligated to resume a relationship with them. Let's assume that a woman has been abused by her husband. She is required by God to forgive her husband, but she isn't required to reconcile with him. It's critical to understand the difference, because many people have taken forgiveness to mean that they must allow people to continue abusing them, which isn't the case.

Once you decide to obey God's Word, the next logical question is how to forgive from a practical perspective. There are a series of steps you can take to ensure you've addressed any unforgiveness that may hide in your life. Though harboring unforgiveness is like taking poison and expecting your enemy to die, that doesn't mean that the person harboring it realizes the poison is there. It eats at you like a disease, affecting your health and every other aspect of your life. The worst part is that while you're experiencing this, the person who wronged you might not know or even care that you're harboring unforgiveness against them. So, who are you really hurting when you don't forgive? Not that person. The best thing to do is to forgive, for your own sake.

How do you know you're harboring unforgiveness toward someone?

- Do you continually rehearse a wrong done to you? Do you mull it over and over in your mind and talk about it to others?

- Are you keeping score? Do you think of ways to get back at the person who wronged you?

- Do you talk about someone negatively? Do you complain about him or her?

- Do you avoid that person?

- Do you continue to hold a grudge, even though someone has asked for forgiveness?

An excellent sign that you're harboring unforgiveness is if you answered yes to any of these questions. However, if you're unsure whether you're holding unforgiveness toward someone, ask God to show you if it's present in your life.

Let me give you some verses of Scripture to think about if you think you might have unforgiveness toward someone but you don't think it's a big enough deal to worry about.

> *"Then Peter came up to him and said, 'Lord, how many times will my brother sin against me and I will forgive him? Up to seven times?' Jesus said to him, 'I do not say to you up to seven times, but up to seventy times seven! 'For this reason the kingdom of heaven may be compared to a man—a king—who wanted to settle accounts with his slaves. And when he began to settle them, someone was brought to him who owed ten thousand talents. And because he did not have enough to repay it, the master ordered him to be sold, and his wife and his children and everything that he had, and to be repaid. Then the slave threw himself to the ground and began to do obeisance to him, saying, 'Be patient with me, and I will pay back everything to you!' So the master of that slave, because he had compassion, released him and forgave him the loan. But that slave went out and found one of his fellow slaves who owed him a hundred denarii, and taking hold of him, he began to choke him, saying, 'Pay back everything that you owe!' Then his fellow slave threw himself to the ground and began to implore him, saying, 'Be patient with me and I will repay you!' But he did not want to, but rather he went and threw him into prison until he would repay what was owed. So when his fellow slaves saw what had happened, they were extremely distressed, and went and reported to their master everything that had happened. Then his master summoned him and said to him, 'Wicked slave! I forgave you all that debt because you implored me! Should you not also have shown mercy to your fellow*

slave as I also showed mercy to you?' And because he was angry, his master handed him over to the merciless jailers until he would repay everything that was owed. So also my heavenly Father will do to you, unless each of you forgives his brother from your hearts!'"
(Matthew 18:21–35, LEB)

Now that we've established the importance of forgiveness, let's talk about the steps to take toward forgiveness.

- Obey God's Word concerning forgiveness. Remember that forgiveness doesn't begin with a feeling: It's a decision we make.

- Pray for your enemies, as commanded in Matthew 5:44.

  "But I say to you, love your enemies and pray for those who persecute you,"
  (Matthew 5:44, LEB)

  You probably won't be able to do this from the heart at first, but keep in mind that this verse doesn't say to pray once. It's an ongoing process, but as you continue to pray for your enemies, you should find the task becomes easier as time passes.

- Don't talk about the matter anymore. Use the same principle of forgiveness that God uses in Psalm 103:12.

  "As far as east is from west, so he has removed far from us the guilt of our transgressions."
  (Psalm 103:12, LEB)

- Meditate on Scriptures that deal with this topic if you struggle with unforgiveness so you can get it deep into your spirit that forgiveness isn't an option. Some key Scriptures are:

"Let all bitterness and wrath and anger and clamor and slander be put away from you, along with all malice. Be kind to one another, tenderhearted, forgiving one another, as God in Christ forgave you."
(Ephesians 4:31–32, ESV)

"And when ye stand praying, forgive, if ye have ought against any: that your Father also which is in heaven may forgive you your trespasses."
(Mark 11:25, KJV 1900)

"Take heed to yourselves. If your brother sins against you, rebuke him; and if he repents, forgive him."
(Luke 17:3, NKJV)

"Do not take revenge yourselves, dear friends, but give place to God's wrath, for it is written, "Vengeance is mine, I will repay," says the Lord."
(Romans 12:19, LEB)

"For we know the one who said, "Vengeance is mine, I will repay," and again, "The Lord will judge his people.""
(Hebrews 10:30, LEB)

"Be ye angry, and sin not: let not the sun go down upon your wrath: Neither give place to the devil."
(Ephesians 4:26–27, KJV 1900)

"And finally, all of you be harmonious, sympathetic, showing mutual affection, compassionate, humble, not repaying evil for evil or insult for insult, but on the other hand blessing others, because for this reason you were called, so that you could inherit a blessing."
(1 Peter 3:8–9, LEB)

"Do not be overcome by evil, but overcome evil with good."
(Romans 12:21, ESV)

"Hatred stirs up strife, but love covers over all offenses."
(Proverbs 10:12, LEB)

"But love ye your enemies, and do good, and lend, hoping for nothing again; and your reward shall be great, and ye shall be the children of the Highest: for he is kind unto the unthankful and to the evil."
(Luke 6:35, KJV 1900)

"Blessed are the merciful: for they shall obtain mercy."
(Matthew 5:7, KJV 1900)

"The understanding of a person makes him slow to his anger, and his glory overlooks offense."
(Proverbs 19:11, LEB)

"If it is possible on your part, be at peace with all people."
(Romans 12:18, LEB)

"bearing with one another, and forgiving one another,
if anyone has a complaint against another;
even as Christ forgave you, so you also must do."
(Colossians 3:13, NKJV)

I find these verses helpful when I'm tempted to hold on to anger and unforgiveness against someone. I hope they'll be of help to you, too. Here's a verse of Scripture that puts that to rest if you're tempted to say that you can't forgive, that the offense is just too big and too hurtful to let go:

"I can do all things through
Christ which strengtheneth me."
(Philippians 4:13, KJV 1900)

Remember that God is a just God, and He would never ask you to do something you can't do, so you can forgive.

Choosing God means you must also choose His ways. He never promises that the road will be easy, but His ways are the right ways, and He demands that we forgive as He has forgiven us. You're opening yourself up to the enemy if you don't forgive. Nothing is worth that.

As this chapter comes to a close, let's review the steps to forgiveness:

- Obey God's Word concerning forgiveness: It's a requirement, not an option.
- Pray for your enemies, as commanded in Matthew 5:44.
- Don't rehearse the matter in your mind or talk about it to others.
- Remember to meditate on verses of Scripture that deal with forgiveness if you struggle with it. You can use the list provided earlier in this chapter.

Here is a prayer you can pray if you have unforgiveness, bitterness, or anger in your life and you'd like to take it to the Lord.

Heavenly Father, I thank you for Your Word. I thank You that within it are the truths I need to lead a successful life. In Joshua 24:15, Joshua told the people to choose which god they would serve. He said that as for him and his household, they would serve the Lord. Father, I choose You. In doing so, I must choose Your ways, and Your ways include the act of forgiveness toward those who have wronged me. I understand it's a requirement and not an option. Your Word says in Mark 11:25 that when I stand praying, I must forgive, that You may forgive my trespasses.

Therefore, I make the commitment to You that I will walk in forgiveness, not only with my Christian brothers and sisters, but with everyone. Father, right now I release any feelings of anger, bitterness, or unforgiveness toward those who have wronged me. Instead, I choose to walk in love and to seek peace all the days of my life. Walking in forgiveness in not a simple thing, so I ask You to help me walk it out. Reveal to me any areas of my life where unforgiveness exists and help me root it out and let it go. Help to see that the forgiveness You extend to me is no less than the forgiveness You expect me to extend to others.

I understand that the act of forgiveness is one of faith and not of feelings. Therefore, I will forgive by faith. I will pray for my enemies as Your Word directs, and I understand that vengeance is Yours, not mine. I will not render evil for evil, but I will put myself in Your hands. I will trust in You.

I forgive others as You have forgiven me. Father, I thank You for helping me to walk out the steps to forgiveness, in Jesus' Name, amen.

You'll find if you're bold enough to pray this payer and take the steps to forgive not only that you become free of the poison unforgiveness brings into your life but also that you've learned the art of forgiveness.

Chapter Eleven: In Times Of Trouble

YOU MUST BE CLEAR ON ONE THING IN ORDER TO BECOME all you need to be as a Christian: You'll have trials and tribulations in this life. That's a promise straight from the Word of God. John 16:33 tells us:

> *"These things I have spoken unto you, that in me ye might have peace. In the world ye shall have tribulation: but be of good cheer; I have overcome the world."*
> *(John 16:33, KJV 1900)*

We see from this verse of Scripture that we will indeed have trouble, but we also see that Jesus has overcome the world. What if I told you that you don't have to face your problems alone? God promises that He will never leave you nor forsake you. That's a promise too, and it's found in Hebrews 13:5.

> *"Your lifestyle must be free from the love of money, being content with what you have. For he himself has said, "I will*

never desert you, and I will never abandon you."'"
(Hebrews 13:5, LEB)

With these Scriptures in mind, what do you do when faced with a problem? We usually respond to the issues of life in the wrong way and never stop to consider a Biblical solution. However, we will look at Scripture in this chapter to find out how we should handle the problems we face.

In 2 Chronicles 20:1-13, it says:

"It came to pass after this also, that the children of Moab, and the children of Ammon, and with them other beside the Ammonites, came against Jehoshaphat to battle. Then there came some that told Jehoshaphat, saying, There cometh a great multitude against thee from beyond the sea on this side Syria; and, behold, they be in Hazazon-tamar, which is En-gedi. And Jehoshaphat feared, and set himself to seek the LORD, and proclaimed a fast throughout all Judah. And Judah gathered themselves together, to ask help of the LORD: even out of all the cities of Judah they came to seek the LORD. And Jehoshaphat stood in the congregation of Judah and Jerusalem, in the house of the LORD, before the new court, And said, O LORD God of our fathers, art not thou God in heaven? and rulest not thou over all the kingdoms of the heathen? and in thine hand is there not power and might, so that none is able to withstand thee? Art not thou our God, who didst drive out the inhabitants of this land before thy people Israel, and gavest it to the seed of Abraham thy friend for ever? And they dwelt therein, and have built thee a sanctuary therein for thy name, saying, If, when evil cometh upon us, as the sword, judgment, or pestilence, or famine, we stand before this house, and in thy presence,

(for thy name is in this house,) and cry unto thee in our affliction, then thou wilt hear and help. And now, behold, the children of Ammon and Moab and mount Seir, whom thou wouldest not let Israel invade, when they came out of the land of Egypt, but they turned from them, and destroyed them not; Behold, I say, how they reward us, to come to cast us out of thy possession, which thou hast given us to inherit. O our God, wilt thou not judge them? for we have no might against this great company that cometh against us; neither know we what to do: but our eyes are upon thee. And all Judah stood before the LORD*, with their little ones, their wives, and their children."*
(2 Chronicles 20:1–13, KJV 1900)

Based on what we read here, what is the first thing that naturally happens when you face unpleasant news? It says that Jehoshaphat felt fear, yet what did he do next? Verse 3 says he "set himself to seek the Lord." This is always Step one.

Let me mention a keyword used here, the word "seek." It isn't a casual term. It has a much deeper meaning than you might think. It means to crave or desire something. Seeking Him requires something from you if you're looking to the Lord for help. It requires you to want His response.

I also want to make sure I drive home another point. Does it say that he ran to ask his family or best friend? No. It says he sought the Lord. Your first response to situations you face shouldn't be going to another person for an answer; your first response should always be to go to God. The sooner you learn that, the sooner you find answers to the problems you face. I heard an expression once that I've been using ever since, and it goes like this: "Run to the throne instead of the phone."

The next several verses will show us how Jehoshaphat sought the Lord. He talked to the Lord about the marvelous things He'd done in the past, and then he spoke to God about the problem. He was authentic. He didn't hide the fact that he couldn't face this problem by himself. He genuinely looked to God for the answer.

Let's find out what happened next. Beginning in verse 14, we read:

"Then upon Jahaziel the son of Zechariah,
the son of Benaiah, the son of Jeiel, the son of Mattaniah,
a Levite of the sons of Asaph, came the Spirit of the LORD
in the midst of the congregation; And he said, Hearken ye,
all Judah, and ye inhabitants of Jerusalem, and thou king
Jehoshaphat, Thus saith the LORD unto you, Be not afraid
nor dismayed by reason of this great multitude; for the
battle is not yours, but God's."
(2 Chronicles 20:14–15, KJV 1900)

God gives us the next step. Step 2 is to fear not. Don't fear. It is perfectly natural to feel fear when you're in trouble, but the key is to not give into it.

Let's continue reading, beginning in verse 16.

"To morrow go ye down against them: behold, they come
up by the cliff of Ziz; and ye shall find them at the end
of the brook, before the wilderness of Jeruel. Ye shall not
need to fight in this battle: set yourselves, stand ye still,
and see the salvation of the LORD with you, O Judah and
Jerusalem: fear not, nor be dismayed; to morrow go out
against them: for the LORD will be with you."
(2 Chronicles 20:16–17, KJV 1900)

What is Step 3? It's listening for God's instructions. God told him exactly what to do. This is key. Follow His instructions precisely when He gives them to you. Do exactly what He says, nothing more and nothing less. This can be difficult to do, especially if He tells you to do something that goes against your natural inclination, yet I emphasize again that you must follow His instructions exactly.

How do you know when God is speaking to you? Sometimes He'll speak to your spirit through the still, small voice about the situation, or you'll have a knowing inside of you regarding a particular direction to take. He might also bring a Scripture to mind that addresses the situation. There are a million unique ways God can speak to you but, regardless of the method He uses, it will bring peace to your mind. Always go with peace.

Remember this: Even if you accidentally veer off track, God will put you back on the right track. Sometimes people think that if they accidentally get off track, God will let them wander off into a ditch, but that's not the case. He knows where to find you and put you back on the right path if you wander off track for any reason. You have his promise on that, and it's found in Proverbs 3:5-6.

"Trust in the LORD with all your heart, And lean not on your own understanding; In all your ways acknowledge Him, And He shall direct your paths."
(Proverbs 3:5–6, NKJV)

I recommend memorizing these verses. He promises that He will guide the steps of a righteous man so you can trust Him to keep His word. Trust that He will lead you and guide you. You might need to wait for an answer, but you'll get an answer. God doesn't always respond right after you ask for help. Waiting is sometimes required, and we need to be clear about that. Don't worry while you're waiting. Trust God.

What's our next step in this process? We see it in the next verses of Scripture, starting in verse 18.

"And Jehoshaphat bowed his head with his face to the ground: and all Judah and the inhabitants of Jerusalem fell before the LORD, worshipping the LORD. And

the Levites, of the children of the Kohathites, and of the children of the Korhites, stood up to praise the Lord *God of Israel with a loud voice on high."*
(2 Chronicles 20:18–19, KJV 1900)

Step 4 is to worship and praise the Lord. We need to understand the difference between worship and praise before we can perform this step correctly. Simply put, worship is to show reverence and adoration for God. Praise is the act of expressing approval or admiration. We can also say it this way: When you worship the Lord, you talk to Him about who He is. When you praise Him, you admire the things He's done. Why is this so important? Because Psalm 22:3 says that God inhabits the praises of His people. You live or dwell in it when you inhabit something, so this verse is saying that God lives and dwells where He is being praised. Start praising Him and see what happens if you want God to arrive on the scene quickly.

Before we move on from this step, it's important to keep in mind that these verses of Scripture don't say to worship and praise God if you feel like it. The last thing you want to do is praise and worship when you're facing a battle, but that's exactly what you should do. In fact, this is what's called "offering up the sacrifice of praise." You can find more information about that in Hebrews 13:15, but we won't be going into detail here.

Let's keep reading in 2 Chronicles, starting with verse 20.

"*And they rose early in the morning, and went forth into the wilderness of Tekoa: and as they went forth, Jehoshaphat stood and said, Hear me, O Judah, and ye inhabitants of Jerusalem; Believe in the* Lord *your God, so shall ye be established; believe his prophets, so shall ye prosper. And when he had consulted with the people, he appointed singers unto the* Lord*, and that should praise the beauty of holiness, as they went out before the army, and to say, Praise the* Lord*; for*

his mercy endureth for ever.”
(2 Chronicles 20:20–21, KJV 1900)

Based on these Scriptures, what is Step 5? It’s obeying what the Lord told you to do. The people went out just like they were told. Let’s see what happened next.

“And when they began to sing and to praise,
the LORD set ambushments against the children of Ammon,
Moab, and mount Seir, which were come against Judah;
and they were smitten.”
(2 Chronicles 20:22, KJV 1900)

Here it says that the Lord set an ambush when they began to sing and praise. Does this remind you of another verse of Scripture we just talked about? Doesn’t it say in Psalm 22:3 that God inhabits the praises of His people? Isn’t that what happened here? The Lord came on the scene as soon as they began to sing and praise. This example is the reason I can’t say enough about how critical praise and worship are when you’re facing an adverse situation.

Let’s read what happened next, starting in verse 23.

“For the children of Ammon and Moab stood up against
the inhabitants of mount Seir, utterly to slay and destroy
them: and when they had made an end of the inhabitants
of Seir, every one helped to destroy another. And when
Judah came toward the watch tower in the wilderness, they
looked unto the multitude, and, behold, they were dead
bodies fallen to the earth, and none escaped.”
(2 Chronicles 20:23–24, KJV 1900)

The armies that came out against King Jehoshaphat and his people ended up destroying each other instead. So, what is Step 6? It’s to continue to praise and worship as you act on His instructions and as you wait for the end of the battle. Verses 24 and 25 tell us the end of this story for King Jehoshaphat.

> *"And when Judah came toward the watch tower in the wilderness, they looked unto the multitude, and, behold, they were dead bodies fallen to the earth, and none escaped. And when Jehoshaphat and his people came to take away the spoil of them, they found among them in abundance both riches with the dead bodies, and precious jewels, which they stripped off for themselves, more than they could carry away: and they were three days in gathering of the spoil, it was so much."*
> (2 Chronicles 20:24–25, KJV 1900)

Now that we've looked at all these verses of Scripture, I want to go back and condense the steps and talk about them in practical terms.

Step 1: Seek the Lord.

- Seeking isn't a casual activity. It means to crave or desire something.
- Don't talk to friends or family first. Go to God first.
- Pray and listen.

Step 2: Do not fear.

- Remember that it is perfectly natural to feel fear, but you shouldn't let that emotion overtake you.

Step 3: Listen for God's instructions.

- God will tell you what you should do when you pray and listen, but also remember that God might not answer your prayer 30 seconds after you pray. You might be required to wait.

- God might tell you to do something strange, but you must not ignore what He instructs you to do, which might include doing nothing at all. Only He knows the outcome of the battle you face, so do what He says without questioning Him about it. And remember that God doesn't deliver by a formula. His instructions will usually be different for each situation. And you can't rely on a set of instructions He gave to someone else. He will customize it for your particular situation.

Step 4: Worship and praise the Lord.

Step 5: Act on God's instructions. Do nothing more, and nothing less.

Step 6: Continue to praise and worship Him as you act on the instructions He's given you and as you wait for the end of the battle.

I realize that it might seem like I'm reducing everything down to a formula by providing a sequence of steps. Please understand that's not my intent. My primary intention is for people to realize that we need to change how we respond to the issues of life. We usually default to the world's way of doing things. We panic, we call Grandma for advice; we beg and negotiate with God to fix our problem or some other type of reaction. However, the Word of God shows us a better way, a way that brings God on the scene.

I also provide this list of steps because it's usually easier to remember that than trying to memorize all the verses of Scripture. Please don't look at this as some checklist to check off, like a list of chores. It's not meant to be like that. It means that we should respect God enough to do things His way. We can expect His result if we do things His way. If packaging these

Scriptures into a set of steps makes it easier for you to respond to life's issues, then that's what I'll do.

Sometimes we need to be reminded that God isn't shocked when things happen. He knows everything before it ever happens. He isn't sitting on His throne saying, "Gee, I wish I had seen that coming." He knows the end from the beginning. Nothing takes Him by surprise.

Remember that while you'll be entangled in battles from time to time, Jesus overcame the world through His death, burial, and resurrection. This means that you're coming up against a defeated foe. Remembering these things can help you to stop and respond to any situation in a way that places your complete trust in God. He will never leave you nor forsake you. He doesn't know how to fail, so trust Him to see you through the trials and tribulations you face.

Chapter Twelve: Fruit Of The Spirit

WE'LL TALK ABOUT THE FRUIT OF THE SPIRIT IN THIS CHAPTER.

"But the fruit of the Spirit is love, joy, peace, patience, kindness, goodness, faithfulness, gentleness, self control. Against such things there is no law."
(Galatians 5:22–23, LEB)

These are thoughts, attitudes, and behaviors that we develop through our walk with God, but they come initially in seed form, so it takes time for them to grow. You don't suddenly become the perfect Christian when you accept Jesus as your Lord and Savior. It doesn't work that way.

The fruit of the Spirit -- love, joy, peace, patience, kindness, goodness, faithfulness, gentleness, and self-control -- are implanted into your spirit at the time you receive Jesus as your Lord and Savior. However, they must be cultivated through study and real-life application, because they don't grow automatically. I encourage Christians, especially new believers, to study the fruit of the Spirit at the beginning of their walk with God, because too many Christians are underdeveloped in these areas, and it renders them ineffective in the kingdom.

Many ministries focus on prosperity, healing, or praying in tongues but leave out the fruit of the Spirit, which is an enormous mistake. Everything needs to be in balance. You can't focus on one area only and then expect to be a mature, developed Christian.

Developing the fruit of the Spirit must be a priority for you to ensure you're everything God needs you to be. Read the verse below carefully.

"Either make the tree good, and his fruit good;
or else make the tree corrupt, and his fruit corrupt: for the
tree is known by his fruit."
(Matthew 12:33, KJV 1900)

This verse says you'll be known by your fruit, so what do your fruit say about you? If you tell people you're a Christian, but then they say something like, "Wow, I wouldn't have guessed that", then you have a problem. You shouldn't even have to tell people you're a Christian. They should see something different about you, something that distinguishes you from the rest of the pagan world. This doesn't mean that you won't make mistakes from time to time, we all do. But your entire personality shouldn't be so worldly that people can't tell the difference between you and the unbeliever down the street.

We are called, as believers in Christ, to bear fruit.

"Every branch in me that beareth not fruit he
taketh away: and every branch that beareth fruit, he
purgeth it, that it may bring forth more fruit."
(John 15:2, KJV 1900)

LOVE

We will begin with love, because it's one of the most important things to learn. Many people think they know what love is. They think they know how to love according to the Word of God, but a believer whose demonstration of love is anything less than what we see in the next few verses is falling short.

> *"Love is patient and kind; love does not envy or boast; it is not arrogant or rude. It does not insist on its own way; it is not irritable or resentful; it does not rejoice at wrongdoing, but rejoices with the truth. Love bears all things, believes all things, hopes all things, endures all things. Love never ends. As for prophecies, they will pass away; as for tongues, they will cease; as for knowledge, it will pass away."*
> (1 Corinthians 13:4–8, ESV)

People use the word "love" all the time, but do they know what it really means? They're angry, mean, hold grudges, and wonder why they're not making an impact in the world. You can't be an example of love if you won't do good things for people. Love isn't for you to say all the time; it's for you to demonstrate to others.

Some people say that they just don't have any love to give, but that's not true for believers. Romans 5:5 says that God's love is shed abroad in our hearts by the Holy Spirit. Since that's the case, we do indeed have love to give. The issue may be that a person hasn't developed in this area.

> *"and hope does not disappoint, because the love of God has been poured out in our hearts through the Holy Spirit who was given to us."*
> (Romans 5:5, LEB)

And if that verse doesn't make my point, the next few will.

"Anyone who does not love does not know God, because God is love."
(1 John 4:8, ESV)

"'A new commandment I give to you: that you love one another—just as I have loved you, that you also love one another. By this everyone will know that you are my disciples—if you have love for one another.'"
(John 13:34–35, LEB)

It takes practice to develop in this area. Love must be part of the deal if you decide to love God with everything you have. This means you must love your neighbor as yourself. It means that you must love your enemies whether or not you want to. Love isn't just a feeling, it's a decision. It's easy to feel love for those who are good to us, but loving an enemy is a whole other thing. It's natural to want to exact revenge if someone has wronged you, but that's not God's way: He demands that we forgive and walk in love. The last thing you feel is the urge to love a person who has wronged you, but the mature believer remembers what the Word of God says and determines to walk in love regardless of how he feels.

If you struggle with walking in love toward someone, then I suggest that you ask God to show you how He sees that person. God has never failed me in this.

An example is when I was struggling once with walking in love toward someone who worked for me. This person was bitter, angry, argumentative, and disrespectful. I wanted to fire him, but the Lord wouldn't let me. He kept telling me to continue walking in love toward him, no matter what. One day, I was so frustrated with this person that I cried before the Lord, "Why do you want me to continue to love him? Don't you see how he acts? Why are you making me put up with this?" The Lord responded by showing me a glimpse of this person's life. He showed me how much disappointment this person had suffered and the issues he was facing at the moment.

The Lord then asked me, "Do you really want to give up so quickly on him? Do you not see that he needs a real demonstration of love? He won't know what it is unless you show him."

I walked away from that conversation with God feeling a great deal of compassion for my employee. It would be a few more years before I saw any actual change in him, but that change was enough to keep me going. I kept at it, with the Lord's help, and today that man is a precious friend of mine. Think of what would have happened if I had been disobedient to the Lord and fired him. I would have missed out on the opportunity to affect his life in a meaningful way. You may not always understand why you're being asked to love someone, but God will show you if you ask Him. Walking in love can be hard, but it's always worth it.

JOY

The joy of the Lord is the only real, lasting joy because it's authentic, and it's in you if you've received Jesus as your Lord and Savior. It doesn't depend on whether times are good or bad. This joy comes from knowing that you're right with God, from knowing that you're going to Heaven to be with the Lord when you die. Genuine joy does not come from things: Your new house, car, or boat do not bring this kind of joy.

This fruit must be developed by walking closely with the Lord. It comes from spending time in prayer, hearing the voice of the Holy Spirit, and doing what the Word says. It comes from a close relationship with God.

The joy of the Lord is your strength (Nehemiah 8:10). It allows you to live in a crazy world without going crazy yourself.

Darkness and fear surround the unsaved. They fear death because they don't know what will happen to them when they die. There's something unsettling about having a conversation with them, because they don't have the guarantee of Heaven when they reach the end of their life.

A believer in Christ who shows the fruit of joy in the presence of the unsaved often causes the lost person to say, "I want what you have. Where can I get some of that?" It draws people to the Lord.

The key to walking in the joy of the Lord is to abide in His presence. It has everything to do with your relationship with God. This joy is possible to achieve for those who focus on Him and put His will first.

"Thou wilt shew me the path of life:
In thy presence is fulness of joy; At thy right hand
there are pleasures for evermore."
(Psalm 16:11, KJV 1900)

This fruit won't be as clear in your life if you don't spend time with the Lord. It'll still be there, but it will largely be dormant.

Here's a real-life example of how this worked for me in the past. I had lost my job because of a corporate acquisition. Once I heard that, I immediately panicked and felt anxiety. I knew enough not to settle for these emotions. I spent some time with the Lord to talk about this situation. The Lord soon told me not to worry and assured me that He already had another job for me. In fact, He even told me not to bother looking for another job, which caused the anxiety to leave. The joy of the Lord arose in its place. It made little sense to feel this way, because the job conditions were grim at that time. Everyone else around me felt depressed, but I knew what my God had said and that He can't lie. I also knew that He would never leave me or forsake me (Hebrews 13:5), so this joy overrode all the other voices.

This is how it can be for you, but you must decide that the voice of the Lord takes precedence over every other voice. It doesn't matter what anyone else says. It doesn't matter what the surrounding circumstances look like. I looked like a complete fool to others for not looking for another job because so few were available. People probably wouldn't find a job if they didn't lie, cheat, and steal to get one. But that's not God's way, and He said to do something different. Thus, you'll get the result He wants for you if you'll do what God says to do. This is how you can walk in the joy of the Lord, even when it makes no sense to anyone else. Yes, you might look crazy in the midst of terrible times, but who cares? If you're doing what the Lord says, it doesn't matter what other people think.

PEACE

The Bible says you'll be known by your fruit (Matthew 12). You receive these fruits if you're a Christian, but the question is whether they've been developed. Peace, which may seem a lot like joy, is actually a different fruit. It's a state in which the believer isn't tormented by fear and anxiety. It's a condition of the heart.

The Lord said in John 14:27:

"Peace I leave with you, my peace I give unto you: not as the world giveth, give I unto you. Let not your heart be troubled, neither let it be afraid."
(John 14:27, KJV 1900)

Jesus came that we may have abundant life (John 10:10), and peace is part of the abundant life. Living in peace isn't a natural state in which to live; it's something that also has to be developed. We are inclined to react with fear, worry, and anxiety when things aren't going perfectly, but there's an antidote to that condition found in Philippians 4:6-7.

"Be anxious for nothing, but in everything by prayer and supplication with thanksgiving let your requests be made known to God. And the peace of God that surpasses all understanding will guard your hearts and your minds in Christ Jesus."
(Philippians 4:6–7, LEB)

John 10:10 and these verses from Philippians are my favorite anti-anxiety scriptures. God will give you peace if you'll give your worries over to Him in return. That's an impressive deal. I do this all the time, and I can tell you that it works, but you have to do it. I've addressed the specific steps to do this effectively in another chapter that deals with anxiety, so I won't belabor it here. Please understand how important it is to live free from anxiety. It's so important that God has made it a requirement rather than a suggestion. You must set your mind to do it, and you must decide to obey this command.

Stop and recall these verses and do what they say to do if you notice you're becoming upset about something. Once you do that and see the results, you'll get into the habit of doing it. It will become a default for you, and then peace can reign in your life.

Colossians 3:15 instructs us to let the peace of God rule in our hearts. It must be the judge of a situation. An example is when a couple is planning to get married. Maybe the woman said yes without thinking about it but doesn't have peace about marrying this person. This situation means something is wrong, and she needs to find out what it is.

Or, let's say you've been job hunting and you receive multiple job offers. One of the job offers seems to be the better of the two. It offers more money, better hours, and a better title. The other offer is less favorable but still seems better than your current job. You really want to take the better offer, but you have a disquieting feeling inside. This means something is wrong because peace isn't reigning in this situation, yet you feel peace deep down inside about accepting the less favorable offer. If peace is reigning in this situation, then that's a clear indicator that you should accept the less favorable offer and pass on the other one. You may never know why the other job wasn't the one for you, but it won't really matter, because the presence of peace is what should drive the decision.

Learning to operate in peace is a sign of maturity. Mature Christians know how to live life in peace even when circumstances aren't going their way. They understand how to pray about a situation according to Philippians 4:6-7 and then leave it in God's hands. They understand, truly understand, that God will never leave or forsake them (Deuteronomy 31:6). Once they hear from God on a matter, they rest in it, knowing He cannot lie.

PATIENCE

You won't learn patience unless you experience situations that challenge it. Many people claim to have patience, but they fall apart when something goes wrong and isn't fixed in five minutes. Patience means waiting on God's timing, but many people say, "Lord, if you don't fix this for me right now, I don't think I can take it." That's not patience. God won't allow you to be tempted beyond your ability to endure it, but He does expect you to endure some trials.

"No temptation has overtaken you
that is not common to man. God is faithful, and he will
not let you be tempted beyond your ability, but with the
temptation he will also provide the way of escape, that you
may be able to endure it."
(1 Corinthians 10:13, ESV)

"These things I have spoken unto you, that in me ye might
have peace. In the world ye shall have tribulation: but be of
good cheer; I have overcome the world."
(John 16:33, KJV 1900)

Many Christians never experience the full plan of God for their life because they refuse to go through the things that will mature them. They think that trials and tribulations are a sign they're doing something wrong, instead of remembering that trials will happen. Persecution is a guarantee.

"And indeed, all those who want to live in a godly manner in Christ Jesus will be persecuted."
(2 Timothy 3:12, LEB)

You'll be one step ahead of most Christians if you can fully grasp that you'll need to endure persecutions in your life. The reason we have so many weak, wimpy Christians in the world is because they don't want to endure any hardship. They think that as Christians they shouldn't have to deal with anything difficult, but this isn't how our Lord and Savior views trials and tribulations. Jesus said in John 17:14-15, *"I have given them thy word; and the world hath hated them, because they are not of the world, even as I am not of the world. I pray not that thou shouldest take them out of the world, but that thou shouldest keep them from the evil."* (John 17:14–15, KJV 1900)

Allow yourself to mature in God, patiently enduring whatever comes your way, and you'll be the kind of Christian that God can use for His purposes.

"But let patience have her perfect work, that ye may be perfect and entire, wanting nothing."
(James 1:4, KJV 1900)

KINDNESS

Just as with any other quality, kindness must be developed. It requires work, but it's worth it because of the witness it provides to the unsaved.

Kindness will draw people to you, but being a bitter, arrogant, angry person will push people away. So, what type of person do you want to be? Demonstrating kindness, even to those who aren't kind to you, is the way to display the qualities and characteristics of Jesus.

Showing kindness to somebody doesn't mean that you let people take advantage of you. It does require you to go the extra mile to be kind, even when you don't want to be. There will be times when you need to draw the line on a situation, but you need to exercise kindness before it gets to that point.

"A person of kindness rewards himself, but
a cruel person harms his own flesh."
(Proverbs 11:17, LEB)

"And be ye kind one to another,
tenderhearted, forgiving one another, even as God for
Christ's sake hath forgiven you."
(Ephesians 4:32, KJV 1900)

"Therefore all things whatsoever ye
would that men should do to you, do ye even so to them:
for this is the law and the prophets."
(Matthew 7:12, KJV 1900)

Kindness must be developed, just as with the other fruit of the Spirit. It's a decision and not a feeling, so decide to be kind, even when you don't feel like it.

GOODNESS

Goodness is described as moral goodness, virtue, or being upright in heart. It's not something that happens automatically; it requires you to decide to do the right thing, no matter what. It requires you not only to stand against the crowd that wants to do the wrong thing, but it also requires you to sometimes do the thing that makes no sense. For example, Matthew 5:44 is one of those verses that's tough to take. Let's look at it together.

"But I say unto you, Love your enemies, bless them that curse you, do good to them that hate you, and pray for them which despitefully use you, and persecute you;"
(Matthew 5:44, KJV 1900)

Another example is Romans 12:21.

"Do not be overcome by evil, but overcome evil with good."
(Romans 12:21, LEB)

You may think when you first look at these verses that doing good is something you do if you feel like it, but it's not. It's a requirement, not a suggestion. Let me say it again: This is something you must do. Jesus wouldn't tell you to do it if you weren't capable of it: It wouldn't be fair for him to tell you to do something you cannot do.

"As we have therefore opportunity, let us do good unto all men, especially unto them who are of the household of faith."
(Galatians 6:10, KJV 1900)

"Recompense to no man evil for evil. Provide things honest in the sight of all men."
(Romans 12:17, KJV 1900)

The entire mission of Jesus was to demonstrate God's goodness throughout the earth and then to sacrifice His life so we can be saved. Let's look at Acts 10:38.

"Jesus of Nazareth—how God anointed him with the Holy Spirit and with power, who went about doing good and healing all who were oppressed by the devil,

because God was with him."
(Acts 10:38, LEB)

Jesus chose to do good every day; thus, this is something we should also seek to do. The question then arises as to how to do good. This comes from knowing the Word of God and doing it. Everything the Word says to do, that's what you do, and don't do it if it says not to do it. This requires that we spend time with the Lord and with His Word. Most people leave their Bible on the coffee table and never open it, except for a few minutes on Sunday. That's not the way this works. Just as you need regular sustenance for your body, you need even more of the Word for your spirit if you decide to live your life the way God intends. That is the only way to walk in this fruit of the Spirit.

I want to leave you with the following verse to ensure you have the correct mindset about goodness.

"Therefore, to the one who knows to do good
and does not do it, to him it is sin."
(James 4:17, LEB)

FAITHFULNESS

Faithfulness is the quality of being loyal and steadfast. It's really about doing what's right, even when there's no benefit to you. It's precious in God's sight, but it's also lacking in today's culture. What does the Bible say about faithfulness? Let's look at Proverbs 28:20 and Luke 16:10.

"A faithful man will abound with blessings, but whoever
hastens to be rich will not go unpunished."
(Proverbs 28:20, ESV)

"One who is faithful in a very little is also faithful in much, and one who is dishonest in a very little is also dishonest in much."
(Luke 16:10, ESV)

The faithful man doesn't care what the crowd does. He isn't swayed by the culture of the day; he's only influenced by the Word of God. He's faithful even when someone isn't faithful to him, and he's faithful even if it costs him something.

We need to understand what it looks like during a normal day to understand how to be faithful. The faithful man shows up to work on time, doesn't take longer breaks than allowed, and doesn't skip out of work before he puts in the required time. He doesn't steal supplies or equipment from his employer, doesn't look for opportunities to shirk his job duties, and puts forth his best effort at all times.

The faithful man keeps his word. If he tells you he'll do something, he does it. He doesn't make excuses. A faithful man who borrows money pays it back. He intends to live up to the terms if he signs a contract.

The faithful married man does not cheat on his wife, even when he thinks he can get away with it. Once he says, "I do", that's the end of his involvement with other women. This man is faithful even when nobody else can see.

The faithful woman functions on the same level.

This fruit of the Spirit must be developed, just like all the others. It doesn't come automatically nor does it come easily. The best way to function in this fruit is to first be faithful to God. You can be faithful to others if you'll determine to be faithful because you love God first. You won't be led astray by the plans and tactics of the enemy if you'll do everything with an eye to pleasing God.

"Whatever you do, work heartily,
as for the Lord and not for men,"
(Colossians 3:23, ESV)

GENTLENESS

Gentleness carries with it the idea of being mild mannered and even tempered. Many people think gentleness is a synonym for weakness, but it's not. It requires a great deal of self-awareness and self-control to be gentle when you'd rather not be. Scripture provides many examples of what gentleness looks like, so let's look at a few, beginning with Proverbs 15:1.

"A soft answer turns away wrath,
but a harsh word stirs up anger."
(Proverbs 15:1, ESV)

The truth of this verse was made real to me when I saw it in action with a person I worked with. A customer came into the office in a terrible mood because a costly mistake had been made on her account. She railed loudly at my co-worker for a couple of minutes. After she stopped to take a breath, my co-worker said to her in a soft voice, "I totally understand and regret that the mistake was made. I will see to it that the issue is resolved right away and we'll ensure it doesn't happen again."

I watched as the customer's countenance immediately changed. She settled down instead of continuing her tirade. After the matter was resolved, the customer said, "I'm really sorry I acted like that. I was really angry. Thank you for helping me."

Somebody might be tempted to say, "Your co-worker had to respond like that. If she'd yelled back at the customer, she would have lost her job."

That's correct, to a certain extent, but it also misses the point. Regardless of the reason my co-worker used that tactic, it still worked.

Her soft answer turned away the customer's wrath, proving the truth of this verse.

Let's look at a few more verses.

"Therefore I, the prisoner in the Lord,
exhort you to live in a manner worthy of the calling with
which you were called: with all humility and gentleness,
with patience, putting up with one another in love, being
eager to keep the unity of the Spirit in the bond of peace;"
(Ephesians 4:1–3, LEB)

"Remind them to be subject to the
rulers and to the authorities, to obey, to be prepared for
every good work, to speak evil of no one, to be peaceable,
gentle, showing all courtesy to all people."
(Titus 3:1–2, LEB)

Remember that gentleness is a requirement and not a suggestion. Everyone who desires to be a fully mature Christian must learn how to function in this fruit. It takes practice, but the results are worth it. Look for every opportunity to demonstrate gentleness to those you come in contact with. You won't regret it.

SELF-CONTROL

Self-control is one of the most difficult fruit to develop for many Christians. It takes self-control to tell the truth when a lie would be more expedient. Self-control is necessary to remain pure before marriage. Refusing to compromise your beliefs even though it will cost you dearly requires self-control. Self-control is essential when faced with any temptation.

"for God gave us a spirit not of fear
but of power and love and self-control."
(2 Timothy 1:7, ESV)

"A breached city where there is no wall is like
a man who has no self-control for his spirit."
(Proverbs 25:28, LEB)

The key to functioning with self-control is remembering that God sees what you're doing when nobody else does. It also requires you to know the behavior that's expected of you. Self-control isn't required if you're allowed to act any way you choose, but it's required when boundaries exist. The only way to know the boundaries is to know what the Word says, but many believers don't read their Bibles. However, ignorance isn't an excuse. Relying on what the culture of the day deems acceptable may run counter to what the Word says, so it's critical for all believers to read their Bible and do what it says. It's a matter of self-control.

"Therefore, to the one who knows to do
good and does not do it, to him it is sin."
(James 4:17, LEB)

The fruit of the Spirit are a critical component of every person's walk with God. They must be developed, just like a muscle. You can't develop your spiritual muscle if you experience no issues. Using a physical example, do you think you'll develop your muscles if you keep lifting the same 5-pound weight you've been lifting for the past ten years? No. You must tax that muscle with a greater weight in order for it to grow. There's no other way.

Look at each test and trial as an opportunity to grow and develop in your walk with God, because operating in these fruits regularly is a hallmark of the mature Christian.

Chapter Thirteen: Be Ye Separate

AS THE WORLD CONTINUES ITS SLIDE INTO MORAL DECLINE, it's becoming harder to convince believers of the truth of God's command in 2 Corinthians 6:17.

"Therefore "come out from their midst and be separate," says the Lord, "and do not touch what is unclean, and I will welcome you,"
(2 Corinthians 6:17, LEB)

In many ways, there's no difference between a believer and an unbeliever if we compare their lives. The unbeliever supports abortion, but so does the believer. The unbeliever embraces New Age doctrines, and so does the believer. The unbeliever drinks, smokes, and fornicates, and so does the believer. The only notable distinction between the two is that the believer goes to church occasionally. That makes no difference if it doesn't affect the outward life.

"But ye have not so learned Christ; If so be that ye have heard him, and have been taught by him, as the truth is in Jesus: That ye put off concerning the former conversation the old man, which is corrupt according to the deceitful lusts; And be renewed in the spirit of your mind; And that ye put on the new man, which after God is created in righteousness and true holiness."
(Ephesians 4:20–24, KJV 1900)

We need to stand out from the rest of the world rather than try to fit in if we're to be effective witnesses. We won't convince anyone that Jesus is the way to go if we walk, talk, and act like everyone else. Paul admonishes believers not to be conformed to the world, which is another way of telling us to remain separate.

"And do not be conformed to this world, but be transformed by the renewing of your mind, that you may prove what is that good and acceptable and perfect will of God."
(Romans 12:2, NKJV)

A genuine experience with Jesus should cause positive changes in our lives. We shouldn't want to do the sinful things we used to do. We should maintain a higher standard based on the truth of God's Word, but many don't know what God's Word says because they don't read it. It has no power to affect your life if it lays unopened on the coffee table.

You may think that your spiritual closets are clean, but I bet we'll find some things that need to be thrown out if we look closely.

Take Halloween, for example. The only purpose for this so-called holiday is to celebrate the satanic new year, yet believers dress up their children as ghouls, goblins, and witches, and never consider the fact that they're paying homage to a demonic entity. Do your research on the purpose of a jack-o'-lantern or bobbing for apples if you've ever wondered about them, because it might make your stomach churn.

Maybe you enjoy the occasional vampire or werewolf movie. Think twice about watching them anymore if you do. Regardless of how romantic the movie may seem, vampires and werewolves are nothing short of demonic, and exposing yourself and your family to these things inoculates you to the spiritual side of this subject. And it's no laughing matter.

You're allowing evil into your home if you watch horror movies. I've heard well-meaning Christians tell me they love the occasional thrill of fear that comes from watching a horror movie. What they're really saying is they welcome the feeling of fear, yet fear isn't from God.

"for God gave us a spirit not of fear
but of power and love and self-control."
(2 Timothy 1:7, ESV)

There are many verses in the Bible that instruct believers not to fear, so we should take that admonition to heart with the movies we watch. You're sadly mistaken if you think it's harmless to expose yourself to fear that comes from entertainment. The psychological effects of watching horror movies can have profound effects, especially on children.

And how about yoga? Churches all across the land have started their own brand of yoga, calling it 'Christian Yoga,' but there's no such thing. Yoga isn't meant to be an exercise program. It's a spiritual practice rooted in Hinduism. You can't separate the exercise from the spiritual components. If you do yoga, you are taking part in Hinduism. It's as simple as that. And lest you think it's harmless to participate in Hinduism, I should mention that it involves the worship of other gods, not the God of the Bible. Stop immediately if you're currently involved in yoga. There are other ways to enjoy good health.

Hypnosis is another area of concern. It's not harmless. The believer must never yield his mind to another person through hypnosis. You don't know the hypnotist's motive, and it doesn't matter if the person claims to be a Christian. Don't yield your mind to someone else. Instead, renew it with the Word of God.

"And be renewed in the spirit of your mind;
And that ye put on the new man, which after God is
created in righteousness and true holiness."
(Ephesians 4:23–24, KJV 1900)

Another unholy practice is the use of angel cards. These cards are supposedly used to communicate with angels and archangels, but they're nothing more than tools for divination, which is expressly forbidden in the Word of God.

"" 'You must not eat anything with the blood; you shall not
practice divination, nor shall you interpret signs."
(Leviticus 19:26, LEB)

Ouija boards are also divination tools. They're not harmless board games, though the manufacturer would try to convince you otherwise. Using a Ouija board can open you up to demonic activity and is prohibited for the child of God because it's a tool for divination.

"There shall not be found among you anyone who makes
his son or his daughter pass through the fire, or one who
practices witchcraft, or a soothsayer, or one who interprets
omens, or a sorcerer,"
(Deuteronomy 18:10, NKJV)

God expressly forbids tattoos in Leviticus 19:28, yet many Christians proudly sport them.

"Ye shall not make any cuttings in your flesh for the dead, nor print any marks upon you: I am the Lord."
(Leviticus 19:28, KJV 1900)

Many people get tattoos without understanding their occult nature. Unknown to many people, some tattoo artists are practitioners of the occult. In fact, the tattoo artist is a priest or shaman in many cultures.

Meditation is another practice of which Christians must be aware. Many people don't know the dangers of New Age meditation or understand that it can be a launching platform for astral projection. Believe it or not, there are Christians who astral project into the second Heaven to do spiritual warfare against principalities. These same folks later need to be delivered from demonic attack, while others never make it out alive. There's no place in the Bible where astral projection is acceptable. It's occultic and must be avoided at all costs.

Returning to the subject of meditation, it's important to distinguish between New Age meditation and the meditation discussed in the Bible, especially in Joshua 1:8.

"This book of the law shall not depart out of thy mouth; but thou shalt meditate therein day and night, that thou mayest observe to do according to all that is written therein: for then thou shalt make thy way prosperous, and then thou shalt have good success."
(Joshua 1:8, KJV 1900)

Biblical meditation involves reflecting on the Word of God, thinking about it deeply. It doesn't include New Age practices, such as guided meditation, breath meditation, Zen meditation, or transcendental meditation. The Christian believer must not take part in these types of meditation because they invite demonic influence and attacks. Meditating on the Word of God causes you to make your way prosperous, whereas meditating any other way could get you into deep trouble. Avoid New Age practices like your life depends on it, because it has destroyed many well-meaning Christians. The Word of God tells us clearly that God's people are destroyed for a lack of knowledge, so we cannot afford to be ignorant of the New Age.

"My people are destroyed for lack of knowledge: Because thou hast rejected knowledge, I will also reject thee, that thou shalt be no priest to me: Seeing thou hast forgotten the law of thy God, I will also forget thy children."
(Hosea 4:6, KJV 1900)

The list of practices discussed so far isn't exhaustive. There are so many other things to avoid, such as the Law of Attraction teachings, spiritual psychology, and gnosticism. For further study on this subject, I heartily recommend the book "The Second Coming of the New Age: The Hidden Dangers of Alternative Spirituality in America and Its Churches" by Steven Bancarz and Josh Peck. The authors were deeply involved in New Age practices before coming to Christ. It's a wonderful book with significant information and warnings for the believer. I especially encourage parents to teach these concepts to their children, because it's a solid guarantee that they'll meet people in school who practice these things, many times not realizing the spiritual danger.

The Word of God specifically states that the believer is to live a life of holiness.

"Because it is written, Be ye holy; for I am holy."
(1 Peter 1:16, KJV 1900)

It's not always easy, but it's worth it. Sometimes we have to choose between making friends or family happy and making God happy. God must come first when it comes to that, and at some point, it will. I offer you the same challenge put forth by Joshua to the Israelites. Choose this day whom you will serve.

"Now therefore fear the Lord, and serve him in sincerity and in truth: and put away the gods which your fathers served on the other side of the flood, and in Egypt; and serve ye the Lord. And if it seem evil unto you to serve the Lord, choose you this day whom ye will serve; whether the gods which your fathers served that were on the other side of the flood, or the gods of the Amorites, in whose land ye dwell: but as for me and my house, we will serve the Lord."

(Joshua 24:14–15, KJV 1900)

Putting God first opens the door to a relationship with Him to which nothing on earth can compare. But it requires you to set yourself apart, because you cannot serve two masters.